For Beth
My Lifelong Companion

CONSTRUCTING
A PUBLIC THEOLOGY

CONSTRUCTING
A PUBLIC THEOLOGY

THE CHURCH IN A PLURALISTIC CULTURE

RONALD F. THIEMANN

WESTMINSTER/JOHN KNOX PRESS
Louisville, Kentucky

Scripture quotations from the Revised Standard Version of the Bible are copyright 1946, 1952, © 1971, 1973 by the Division of Christian Education of the National Council of the Churches of Christ in the U.S.A. and are used by permission.

Book design by Publishers' WorkGroup

First edition

Published by Westminster/John Knox Press
Louisville, Kentucky

PRINTED IN THE UNITED STATES OF AMERICA

2 4 6 8 9 7 5 3 1

Library of Congress Cataloging-in-Publication Data

Thiemann, Ronald F.
  Constructing a public theology : the church in a pluralistic culture / Ronald F. Thiemann. — 1st ed.
      p.   cm.
  Includes bibliographical references and index.
  ISBN 0-664-25130-7

  1. Theology. 2. Social ethics. I. Title.
BT80.T48   1991
230—dc20   91-15204

CONTENTS

ACKNOWLEDGMENTS

Grateful acknowledgment is given for permission to reprint the following copyrighted material:

"Radiance and Obscurity in Biblical Narratives," in *Scriptural Authority and Narrative Interpretation,* ed. Garrett Green. Copyright © 1987 by Fortress Press. Used by permission of Augsburg Fortress Publishers.

"The Unnamed Woman at Bethany," *Theology Today* 44, no. 2 (July 1987). Reprinted by permission of *Theology Today.*

"The Significance of Karl Barth for Contemporary Theology," *The Thomist* 50, no. 4 (October 1986). Reprinted by permission of *The Thomist.*

"Piety, Narrative, and Christian Identity," *Word & World* 3, no. 2 (Spring 1983). Reprinted by permission of *Word & World.* Copyright © 1983 by Luther Northwestern Theological Seminary.

"The Future of an Illusion: An Inquiry into the Contrast Between Theological and Religious Studies," *Theological Education* 26, no. 2 (Spring 1990). Reprinted by permission of *Theological Education.*

"The Scholarly Vocation: Its Future Challenges and Threats," *Theological Education* 24, no. 1 (Autumn 1987). Reprinted by permission of *Theological Education.*

PREFACE

The essays in this volume represent some initial explorations into the complicated question of religion's role in contemporary public life. My interest in these issues was originally spawned by the civil rights movement of the late 1950s and early 1960s. Though that movement corresponded with my late childhood and early adolescence, it still awoke in me a sense that my Christian faith had genuine relevance for matters of justice in public life. I vividly recall observing the march on Washington on my family's small black-and-white television set and experiencing intense religious and political emotions as I sat, transfixed, listening to Dr. King's "I Have a Dream" speech. John F. Kennedy's powerful rhetoric evoked a sense of civic responsibility during my high school years, and my heightened political consciousness was refined through vigorous discussion with my closest high school friend, Mel Piehl, now Professor of American History at Christ College, Valparaiso University. Chapter 1 of this volume, "Toward an American Public Theology: Religion in a Pluralistic Democracy," was originally developed as the O. P. Kretzmann Lecture at Valpo, an occasion that allowed the rekindling of a long-interrupted conversation with an old and dear friend.

The assassinations of the Kennedy brothers, Dr. King, and Malcolm X and the tragedy of the Vietnam War led me to a brief flirtation with radical politics and a longer period of uncertainty about the relation of faith and public life. During this time I decided to enter the Christian ministry and began my preparation for a theological vocation. My ability to think theologically and politically was decisively shaped during this period by my vigorous debates with Gilbert Meilaender, now Professor of Christian Ethics at Oberlin College. Although we disagree about almost every issue imaginable, we have sustained a remarkable intellectual and personal friendship for the past twenty-five years. Though he finds my political liberalism wrong-headed and my Christian orthodoxy suspect, he has remained my most important teacher and sustained critic. His influence is explicitly acknowledged in Chapter 6, "Worship and Public Responsibility," but is implicitly present throughout the volume.

My years of doctoral study at Yale and Tübingen yielded a dissertation on the Christological debates between Karl Barth and Werner Elert during the tumultuous period of German politics from 1932 through 1936. In doing the research for that work, I discovered that Elert, the theologian most revered by my teachers at Concordia Seminary, was deeply sympathetic to some aspects of the Nazi ideology and saw no conflict between his convictions as a Lutheran theologian and his tacit support for the Nazi regime. My desire to understand more clearly the profound political blindness of my own Lutheran tradition led me to a serious study of the period of the late Weimar Republic and the early Third Reich. During my ten years of teaching at Haverford College, I regularly offered a course on the German Church Struggle and the Holocaust, and I continue my active involvement in Jewish-Christian relations. Chapter 4 of this volume, "Karl Barth and the Task of Constructing a Public Theology," represents my attempt to relate these issues to the contemporary American scene. My insights on these matters are deeply indebted to my beloved teacher, the late Hans Frei, who, though he wrote very little about religion and politics, taught me much of what I know about this subject.

My move to the deanship of Harvard Divinity School in 1986 corresponded with a renewed scholarly interest in the issue of the public significance of theological discourse. My previous book, *Revelation and Theology: The Gospel as Narrated Promise,* was published a few months after the appearance of George Lindbeck's influential *The Nature of Doctrine,* and many reviewers noted the formal similarities between Lindbeck's "postliberal" theology and my nonfoundational "descriptive" theology. Other critics thought they saw a connection between my work and that of Stanley Hauerwas, given our common interest in the category of "narrative," and they raised the question of whether my theological position was relevant to the world of common and public human experience. I began to pursue inquiry into the topic of public theology both as a way of answering my critics and as a means of distinguishing my work from that of Professors Lindbeck and Hauerwas. While I remain indebted to both of them, my own instincts about the relevance of theology for public life are importantly different. The introduction and Chapter 2 serve most directly to sketch my own distinctive position on the questions of biblical narrative, descriptive theology, and public life.

These essays have been markedly improved by the careful and vigorous critique of my colleagues and friends. Conversations with the following colleagues have been particularly important in shaping my thinking on the question of religion in public life: Constance Buchanan, Harvey Cox, Mark Edwards, Francis Schüssler Fiorenza, Walter Fluker, Robert Franklin, Bryan Hehir, George Hunsinger, Jon Levenson, William Placher, Michael Root, Elisabeth Schüssler Fiorenza, and William Werpehowski. I leave it to the discerning reader to discover the influence of such a wonderfully diverse group of colleagues upon my work! I am profoundly grateful for the help and counsel of these friends, and yet I am acutely aware that these essays are at best early explorations into an enormously complex subject. The task of constructing a public theology is a genuinely collaborative effort, and I look forward to continued opportunities to engage in common work on this important topic. Such work within theological education has been tirelessly encouraged by the Lilly Endowment through the able leadership of Bob Lynn and Craig Dykstra. Because of their support and encouragement, I have been able to carry on a scholarly program even as I exercised my primary administrative responsibilities. I am deeply grateful to the Endowment for helping me to protect that endangered species, the scholar-administrator.

The essays in this volume represent scholarly work that has emerged from my research and teaching during the past fifteen years. This professional work has been sustained, embraced, and nurtured by a personal relationship that has provided a constant source of support for more than twenty-three years. I met my wife, Beth, when we were both seventeen years old, and we were married at age twenty-one. While I would undoubtedly be appalled if either of my daughters, Sarah or Laura, entered into marriage at such a tender age, I will be forever grateful that I have been able to share so much of my life with this remarkable woman. We have grown together through the decades, and we have fashioned a common bond that knits together the public and personal dimensions of our lives. She has taught me much about patience and compassion, about teaching and learning, about hospitality and friendship. If there is a single theme that unites the essays in this book, it is the importance of the virtue of hope. My relationship with Beth has provided a constant source of both joy and love, and I dedicate this volume to her as an expression of our shared hope in the future of our lifelong journey of companionship.

June 1991
Cambridge, Massachusetts

INTRODUCTION

Consider the following three situations:

1. You are the pastor of a working-class congregation in a small city in the Midwest. Your community has been relatively stable for nearly three generations, the economy is fairly strong, and many young people enter the work force immediately following high school. Your congregation, which grew dramatically during the 1950s and early 1960s, is growing older, and membership is diminishing as you struggle to keep the young people involved in the life of the church.

One day you receive a call from the mother of a teenage girl asking you to see them both on the next day. The mother is a lifelong member of the congregation, a regular participant in the church's worship and social life. The daughter was baptized in the church, attended Sunday School faithfully, was confirmed, but has been irregular in her involvement during her teenage years. When they arrive for their appointment, you can tell that the daughter has come under duress and that both mother and daughter are in an emotionally distraught state. The mother tells you that the daughter is pregnant and wants to have an abortion. The mother, believing that abortion is an act of killing, is opposed to abortion on religious grounds. She wants the daughter to carry the baby to term, deliver the child, and raise it within their extended family. The daughter, pleading with you to reason with her mother, says that her life will be ruined if she has to continue the pregnancy. "Doesn't anyone care about me?" she asks. "Doesn't God care about my life, too?"

How do you seek resolution to this conflict? Should the wishes of the daughter and the mother weigh equally in your advice? What biblical and theological resources would you use to help mediate this con-

15

flict? Should your own personal position on abortion influence your advice?

2. You are the vice-chair of the church council of a multiethnic urban congregation in the state capital. Many members of the congregation are involved in state and local politics, and the church has a long history of social outreach to the community. Because members of both major political parties belong to the church, there have been some tensions within the congregation, but the church members have been noted for their ability to work together harmoniously. The president of your church council, Ray Jones, has recently been elected to the state senate. A prominent businessman in the community, he and his family have been members of the congregation for nearly twenty years. An active supporter of the Republican party, he has been a major fund-raiser both for the party and for the parish. He decided to enter politics because of his concern about the declining morality of American public life. He is convinced that religious convictions can play an important role in helping shape policies for the state. Shortly after his election, he introduces a bill to the senate seeking the reinstatement of the death penalty for capital crimes. He gives an impassioned speech, which is given wide coverage by the local media, in which he argues for the death penalty on both moral and religious grounds. Quoting regularly from the Bible, he argues that retributive justice is an essential aspect of a just and orderly society. To your surprise, many members of your congregation rally to support Mr. Jones and his bill. An equal number of persons, however, deplore his position and demand his resignation as president of the church council. Unfortunately, the division within the church on this issue also falls along racial lines, and the possibility for a major schism within the congregation is very real. A meeting has been called for this evening to discuss the situation.

As vice-chair of the council, you will chair the meeting and introduce the issues. What is the proper leadership role for you to take? You are convinced on religious and moral grounds that capital punishment is wrong. Should you seek to convince the congregation of the rightness of your position, knowing that taking one side of the dispute could guarantee a schism? How do you balance the demands of your personal beliefs and your role as representative of the entire congregation?

3. Members of your congregation, Mr. and Mrs. Smith, are professionals in their mid-thirties, the parents of two children. Both parents have had leadership positions in the church and are very active in the congregation's ministry. Seven months ago, Mrs. Smith unexpectedly be-

came pregnant, and after much discussion with the family and with you, Mrs. Smith decided to carry the child to term. You receive a phone call from the hospital informing you that Mrs. Smith went into labor and has delivered a premature baby. The infant has been diagnosed as having Down's syndrome, with the added complication of an intestinal blockage. The latter can be corrected with a simple operation; without the surgery, the child cannot be fed and will die.

The day after the delivery, in consultation with the physician, both parents agreed that they did not want to raise the child and refused to give permission for the corrective operation on the intestinal block. They argue that it would be unfair to the other children in the household to raise them with a Down's syndrome child. At a meeting with you and the Smiths, the physician explained that the degree of retardation cannot be predicted at birth. Down's syndrome, he asserted, is one of the milder forms of mental retardation. Downs children usually have IQs in the 50–80 range and sometimes even higher. They can often hold simple jobs, and they are usually very happy children and can be a great joy to the family. The Smiths remain firm in their conviction not to have the surgery performed, and the doctor informs them that he will seek a court order mandating the operation.

As pastor of the congregation, can you play a role in mediating this dispute? Should the parents' wishes be respected above everything else? Should your own judgment about the morality of the situation influence the counsel you give the Smiths? Is this a situation that only the courts can resolve?[1]

These three cases, depicting circumstances increasingly common within contemporary Christian life, illustrate some of the difficulties Christians face in living lives shaped by the gospel in today's culture. Although the moral and theological deliberations required by these situations would have been difficult at any time, they seem particularly vexing in our current cultural situation. The dilemmas presented in these cases seem especially intractable because of our inability to agree on the beliefs, principles, and premises that should guide our moral reasoning. And even if we discern the proper principles, their application to the particular situation often remains unclear.

How does the Christian commandment to love apply in the case of the pregnant young woman? Given the Christian obligation to provide special care to those who are most vulnerable, whose welfare should take precedence, that of the teenage girl or that of the fetus/unborn child?

How does one acknowledge the obligation to respect the young woman's freedom to decide and still recognize the importance of the family setting within which a responsible decision must be made? To what extent do factors external to the resources of the Christian community (e.g., the legal status of abortion or the importance of the women's movement) affect your judgment in this case? To what extent should such factors influence Christian decision making?

What is required of those who provide leadership within Christian congregations? Should the vice-chair of the congregation in the second case take a role of advocacy or reconciliation in seeking to resolve the crisis in the parish? Should her personal convictions on the question of capital punishment influence her leadership role? How does the question of racial division within the congregation affect the advocacy/reconciliation decision? How, if at all, might biblical and theological resources assist you in stating the issues for the congregation? Do you consider Mr. Jones's use of biblical warrants in bolstering his case for capital punishment to be justified? Should you seek to make a counter biblical case in order to refute his position?

What Christian moral principles would you appeal to in counseling the Smiths? Should questions of the quality of human life play any role in Christian decision making? How does one adjudicate the conflict between "sanctity of life" and "quality of life" considerations? Is the refusal to allow surgery an act of infanticide? Is there a morally relevant distinction between "letting die" and "killing" in this case? Would your moral reasoning regarding life-saving surgery change if the life of an infirm elderly person were at stake? Why or why not? How do you react to the doctor's decision to take this matter to the courts? Should the state become involved in questions of personal decision making?

THE SEARCH FOR
AN AUTHENTIC PUBLIC VOICE

We live at a time and in a culture in which we have little societal agreement concerning some of the most basic moral questions. Moral pluralism not only characterizes the broader society; it has also taken root within the churches and within our own souls. Contemporary Christians are socialized into a world littered with the fragments of previously coherent traditions and formerly intact communities. Our identities and moral sensibilities are shaped not by any single cultural framework, but by the bits and pieces of skill, wisdom, and insight we discover along life's way. It is little wonder, then, that many Christians, when faced with the complicated demands inherent in such cases as these, are plagued by moral paralysis and seek a retreat from moral decision making.

These cases not only illustrate the conflicting demands that characterize contemporary Christian decision making; they also reveal the inevitable public dimension of situations that once might have been considered to be purely private. Although decisions regarding abortion and the care of handicapped newborns are intensely personal, they are influenced by contexts that are public and political in nature. The line between private and public, between the personal and the political, can no longer be drawn with absolute clarity. If moral decision making has an inevitable political dimension, then moral and theological reflection must seek to assist Christians in dealing with the public aspects of their lives.

This volume seeks to show that a theology shaped by the biblical narratives and grounded in the practices of the Christian community can provide resources to enable people of faith to regain a public voice in our pluralistic culture. Our challenge is to develop a public theology that remains based in the particularities of the Christian faith while genuinely addressing issues of public significance. Too often, theologies that seek to address a broad secular culture lose touch with the distinctive beliefs and practices of the Christian tradition. In their zeal to engage a public realm in which theological discourse is either unknown or viewed with suspicion, theologians tend to adopt concepts and forms of analysis foreign to the Christian faith. In the process, the distinctive substance and prophetic "bite" of the Christian witness are undermined. On the other hand, theologies that seek to preserve the characteristic language and patterns of Christian narrative and practice too often fail to engage the public realm in an effective and responsible fashion. Either they eschew public discourse altogether in order to preserve what they see as the uniqueness of Christian life, or they enter the public fray with single-minded ferocity, heedless of the pluralistic traditions of our democratic polity. If Christians are to find an authentic public voice in today's culture, we must find a middle way between these two equally unhappy alternatives.

THE CRITERIA FOR
A CHRISTIAN PUBLIC THEOLOGY

Although there is general agreement among contemporary theologians that the Christian faith has public or political implications, there is very little consensus regarding the proper form for a Christian public theology. Indeed, theologians remain sharply divided on the question of the criteria for a genuine public theology.

In his influential book *The Analogical Imagination*, David Tracy has set forward an extensive proposal regarding the public character of theology.[2] Tracy identifies three "publics" relevant to the theologian's work: society, the academy, and the church. Each public situation obliges the theologian to make explicit the "criteria, evidence, warrants, disciplinary status" of his or her work.[3] Only by acceding to this "demand for publicness" can the theologian forfend that dreadful "retreat from the realm of polity . . . to the sphere of our private lives where 'personal preferences' are still allowed to reign."[4] "The theologian," Tracy further asserts, "should argue the case (pro or con) on strictly public grounds that are open to all rational persons."[5] "Personal faith or beliefs," therefore, "may not serve as warrants or support for publicly defended claims to truth. Instead, some form of philosophical argument (usually either implicitly or explicitly metaphysical) will serve as the major warrant and support for all such claims."[6] In making such metaphysical assertions, the theologian "discloses permanent possibilities for human existence both personal and communal."[7]

Tracy's criteria for genuine public theology are thus threefold. All theological proposals must (1) make the structure and logic of argument explicit, (2) present arguments available to all rational persons, (3) provide philosophical warrants of sufficient generality to show that the theological position is grounded not in the particulars of faith or belief but in some possibility available to human existence generally.

Although I am in complete agreement with Tracy's first criterion, I have a concern about the second and find the third and final criterion unacceptable. Certainly, every theologian must make the data, warrants, and backings of theological argument available for public examination. Any appeal to hidden or private sources of authority or justification is inappropriate for a genuinely public theology. The structure and logic of theological argument must be available for examination by any reasonable inquirer. When understood in that sense, I am also in agreement with Tracy's second criterion. But when he uses the phrase "all rational persons" and argues further for the necessity of a general philosophical argument that reveals a possibility available to human existence per se, my concerns begin to surface.

I have written at length in previous works about the difficulties and dangers of arguments that seek to show that religion or faith is a permanent possibility for human existence.[8] I do not believe that the kind of metaphysical argument Tracy demands can be consistently or coherently formulated.[9] If that is so, then Tracy's final criterion demands the impossible of Christian theology and thereby renders the task of public theology hopeless. Moreover, by identifying genuine publicness with general philosophical argument, Tracy undercuts the ability of Christians to employ the specific resources of their traditions to engage in public conversation. Any use of the particular convictions and practices of the Christian community would apparently constitute an appeal to "personal faith or beliefs" that, according to Tracy, cannot be used as warrants in public argument. Tracy's third criterion thus threatens to render the distinctive content of Christian belief inapplicable to the public sphere.[10]

Tracy's desire to ground theology's publicness in general philosophical or metaphysical argument has the further effect of distancing theological reflection from the particular policy dilemmas that so bedevil public life today. Although such arguments might be of interest to the diminishing number of academics concerned with metaphysical speculation, they seem to have little relevance to the situations described at the outset of this introduction.[11] In order to relate the Christian faith to issues like abortion, capital punishment, and the treatment of handicapped newborns, we need to gain a detailed understanding of the social, cultural, and moral context within which public policies are developed. We need to engage in what Clifford Geertz has called "thick description," a process of inquiry that begins with "exceedingly extended acquaintances with extremely small matters" and moves slowly and cautiously to "broader interpretations and abstract analyses."[12]

A "THICK DESCRIPTION"

The form of public theology I wish to defend in this volume takes its rise from the specific beliefs, rituals, and practices of the Christian community. Public theology is not a specialized discipline or a technical subspecies with a unique method of inquiry. Like all Christian theology, it is guided by the Anselmian credo "I believe in order that I may understand." Public theology is faith seeking to understand the relation between Christian convictions and the broader social and cultural context within which the Christian community lives. In order for that relation to be properly understood, the theologian must offer a careful and detailed "thick description" of the entities being compared. The goal is not to provide an overarching theory that explains how "church and world" or "fundamental question and answer" are related to one another. Rather, the goal is to identify the particular places where Christian convictions intersect with the practices that characterize contemporary public life.

The kind of public theology I am proposing does not seek answers to questions like: "Has existence any ultimate meaning? Is a fundamental trust to be found amidst the fears, anxieties, and terrors of existence? Is there some reality, some force, even some one who speaks a word of truth that can be recognized and trusted?"[13] Because public theology begins from the standpoint of faith, the theologian launches his or her inquiry with the conviction that those questions have been answered positively through the revelation of God in Jesus Christ. The theologian thus enters the public realm with the confidence, born of faith, that Christian convictions do have relevance for public life. But *how* those convictions relate to the complicated patterns of social, political, and institutional life cannot be known in advance. How Christians should relate to liberal democracy, a capitalist economy, and a secularized consumer society can only be determined through careful comparative study. The particular relevance of Christian convictions for issues like abortion, capital punishment, and medical care for handicapped newborns must be discovered through a process of rigorous inquiry in which faith risks genuine engagement with the forces of public life.

The definition of theology I offer in Chapter 7 of this volume provides a useful orientation to the task of public theology.

> The theologian speaks from within the community of believers and thus speaks from the commitment of faith. The theologian cannot adopt a standpoint of radical doubt or assume a hypothetical position of neutrality vis-à-vis the Christian faith. The theologian is seeking neither to justify nor disconfirm that complex phenomenon we call faith. The theologian strives simply to *understand* through critical reflection. The process of understanding may yield a radical criticism and reinterpretation of tradition, or it may result in a confirmation of many ancient formulas. The outcome of theological investigation cannot be predicted in advance precisely because the theologian operates within the temporal ebb and flow of history and community. But the goal of theology remains constant, namely, to understand more fully and more critically the Christian faith in order that the community might better exemplify the Christian identity to which it has been called. . . . Informed by Christian practice, yet critically reflecting upon it, the theologian seeks to articulate the gospel so that through it God might mold our Christian identity. Informed by theology, yet not determined by it, the Christian community continues to be a tradition, an ongoing conversation about the nature of Christian faith and life.[14]

Public theology is a genuine risk-taking venture. By opening the Christian tradition to conversation with those in the public sphere, public theology opens Christian belief and practice to the critique that inevitably emerges from those conversation partners. Though I do not find the term "correlation" useful in describing the method of public theology, I am committed to the "mutual criticism" that David Tracy has identified as a natural concomitant of theological involvement in public life.[15]

The standpoint of faith does not make the theologian or the Christian community immune from criticism. On the contrary, because the starting point for public inquiry is faith rather than rational demonstration or transcendental argument, entrance into the public sphere is filled with genuine risk, including the possibility that some of the community's most basic convictions might have to be reformed or even jettisoned. Such radical reshaping of the tradition should take place only after prolonged and rigorous inquiry, but openness to that possibility is an essential element of a faith that honestly seeks critical understanding.[16]

THE CHRISTIAN COMMUNITY, A COMMUNITY OF HOPE

It will be evident to those familiar with the contemporary theological scene that my position bears some resemblance to that of the so-called postliberal theologians.[17] In my book *Revelation and Theology: The Gospel as Narrated Promise,* I argue that Christian theology ought to be both "nonfoundational" and "descriptive," eschewing general explanatory schemes and seeking to provide a "justification of Christian belief [that] is specific to the Christian faith, community, and tradition. . . . Nonfoundational theology is located squarely within Christian tradition and community and seeks to 're-describe' the internal logic of the Christian faith."[18]

Although I share with colleagues like George Lindbeck and Stanley Hauerwas many common assumptions about the theological task, it is important in this context to identify some important differences among us.[19]

Although both Lindbeck and Hauerwas appear willing to adopt the designation "postliberal," I find myself acutely uncomfortable with that label. Our contemporary social and cultural situation is sufficiently complex to resist easy categorization. In addition, at a time when liberalism is under attack from critics on both ends of the political spectrum, theologians would be well advised not simply to join the chorus of antiliberal voices. If one goal of descriptive, nonfoundational theology is to preserve a distinctive Christian voice in a pluralistic conversation, then it is important that the categories of analysis employed by Christian public theology maintain some conceptual independence from nontheological forms of analysis. I am concerned that Stanley Hauerwas's continued attack on liberalism as the "politics that know not God" blinds him to the resources that liberalism might provide for the reconstruction of a political ethos that honors the pluralism of contemporary public life.[20] A more careful "thick description" of liberalism will, I believe, allow for a more nuanced engagement of Christian theology with America's predominant political philosophy. Although I find George Lindbeck to be more circumspect in his judgments about the current cultural and political climate, I fear that his pessimistic reading of our postmodern culture will engender such skepticism about the possibility of Christian involvement in public life as to render a public theology virtually impossible.[21]

I take public theology to be a natural concomitant of theology's descriptive, critical, and constructive tasks. A careful description of the fabric of Christian thought and practice requires attention to the broader social and cultural setting within which Christians seek to live lives shaped by the gospel. As my brief case studies have shown, Christian vocation is most often worked out in the complex and ambiguous joints between "church and world." If descriptive theology genuinely seeks to assist Christians in the formation of the dispositions, capacities, and skills characteristic of discipleship, then it must attend to the public dimensions of Christian life. Contemporary Christians face a bewildering array of contexts within which they are called to manifest the virtues of Christian discipleship. Although theology cannot anticipate every new challenge that contemporary society might cast before the Christian community, it does have a responsibility to provide some specific guidance regarding the relation, for example, between discipleship and citizenship in a liberal democracy. The goal should not be the simple recommendation of one form of life over the other, but a careful and critical analysis of the variety of ways the two might interact. Inquiry into public policies regarding the poor might call forth a vigorous Christian critique of current governmental practice. Analyses of the acquisitive individualism of the consumer culture might evoke a Christian witness to a form of communal life unknown to most people in our society. A careful examination of the liberal tradition's ability to foster a social environment in which persons with diverse commitments can live together without resort to violence might lead to a Christian defense of some current political arrangements.[22] A public theology that is authentically descrip-

24

tive and nonfoundational must engage in careful and detailed comparative analysis of the complex web of relations within which Christians
work out their vocation to discipleship.

I argue throughout the chapters in this volume that one of the most
important political tasks for the contemporary Christian community is to
be a community of hope in a culture that is increasingly cynical about our
common human future. Broadside attacks on liberalism or cultural despair about our de-Christianized society do not function to nurture a
sense of hope about God's reconciling action in behalf of the entire cosmos. Indeed, these approaches can have the unintended but devastating
consequence of discouraging Christians from engaging in positive political action in the public realm. But if persons formed in those communities in which the virtues of faith, hope, and love are nurtured fail to
manifest those virtues in public life, then the *polis* will indeed be left to
those with a shrunken and desiccated view of the possibilities of political
community. Then the accusation that liberalism represents the "politics
that know not God" will be not a description of public life but a self-
fulfilling prophecy. My hope is that a Christian public theology will contribute not to the death of liberal democracy but to its moral renewal.

The chapters of this volume mark the first steps in my own effort to
exemplify the kind of theology I have advocated in this Introduction. I
recognize that I have not yet achieved the full "comparative thick description" that would be necessary in order to address the complicated moral
dilemmas with which I began this study. This volume seeks rather to
point the way *toward* such a fuller effort by showing how careful attention
to the form and substance of biblical narratives, the practices of Christian
worship and piety, the institutional life of church and the academy, and
the pluralism of contemporary society can contribute to the descriptive,
critical, and reconstructive task of a public theology. The achievement of
a public theology adequate to the challenge posed by contemporary society will require a collaborative effort by persons in a variety of disciplines,
including persons in professional life outside of the academy. If this volume encourages others to become involved in this act of Christian faith
and hope, then my effort might indeed be a contribution toward *Constructing a Public Theology*.

NOTES

1. This case is adapted from the "Johns Hopkins Hospital case" as presented in James M. Gustafson, "Mongolism, Parental Desires, and the Right to
Life," *Perspectives in Biology and Medicine* 17 (Summer 1973): 529–530.

25

2. David Tracy, *The Analogical Imagination* (New York: Crossroad, 1981).

3. Ibid., 21.

4. Tracy, *Analogical Imagination,* 10.

5. Tracy, *Analogical Imagination,* 64.

6. David Tracy and John B. Cobb, Jr., *Talking About God* (New York: Seabury Press, 1983), 9. For other works in which Tracy discusses the public responsibility of the theologian, see *Plurality and Ambiguity* (San Francisco: Harper & Row, 1987) and "Defending the Public Character of Theology," *Christian Century* 98 (April 1, 1981): 350–356.

7. Tracy, *Analogical Imagination,* 14.

8. See Ronald F. Thiemann, *Revelation and Theology: The Gospel as Narrated Promise* (Notre Dame: University of Notre Dame Press, 1985), esp. 3–6, 17–46, 186–188; "Revelation and Imaginative Construction," *Journal of Religion* 61, no. 3 (July 1981): 242–263; "G. E. Lessing: An Enlightened View of Judaism," *Journal of Ecumenical Studies* 18, no. 3 (Summer 1981): 401–422. For similar arguments in the chapters in this volume, see Chapters 2, 4, 7, and 8.

9. As I argue in the works cited in n. 8, I believe that all such metaphysical or transcendental arguments inevitably fall victim to the conceptual incoherence associated with epistemological foundationalism. For a listing of the most important works on epistemological foundationalism, see Chapter 2, n. 8.

10. This brief summary and critique of Tracy's sophisticated and nuanced argument hardly does justice to the rich fabric of his presentation. In particular, I have not given sufficient attention to the way in which Tracy argues for distinct forms of publicness within fundamental, systematic, and practical theologies.

It is clear that Tracy will allow for the use of particular Christian warrants in the latter two forms of theology *as long as they are related to claims justifiable by fundamental theology.* Tracy's commitment to a disclosure model of truth within all three publics grants inevitable priority to fundamental theology within his entire theological scheme. Fundamental theology establishes the universal presence of the "genuinely 'religious' question, that is, a fundamental question of the meaning of human existence" (*Analogical Imagination,* 61) and seeks a "mutual critical correlation" between "fundamental questions and answers which any attentive, intelligent, reasonable and responsible person can understand and judge" (61). The systematic theologian then seeks to show how the symbols of a particular faith tradition "disclose permanent possibilities of meaning and truth" through that tradition's classic texts. Systematic theology is public theology insofar as its texts are de facto "cultural classics." "The notion of a religious classic as a cultural classic can assure the entry of all theological classics into the public realm of culture." If this were not so, "systematic theology would be eliminated" as a form of public discourse (68–69.) The public status of systematic theology is thus grounded in its relation to fundamental theology. The same is true for the public status of practical theology. Practical theologians are engaged in public theology because, like the practitioners of the other two forms of theological inquiry, they are engaged in a mutual correlation of "those fundamental questions constituting religious questions and those fundamental responses constituting particular religious traditions" (81). Practical theologies participate in the disclosive possibility established by fundamental theology. "Theologies of liberation," Tracy argues, "represent above all a classic event in search of a classic text. . . . They represent . . . the liberating reality of a classic, a kairotic event disclosing and transforming all" (397–398).

As I have argued in the works cited in n. 8, I remain skeptical of the possibility of fundamental theology as Tracy conceives of it. (For a more modest, and I believe ultimately more successful, form of fundamental theology, see Francis Schüssler Fiorenza, *Foundational Theology* [New York: Crossroad, 1984].) Consequently, I cannot accept either the priority Tracy grants to fundamental theology or his particular understanding of the "method of correlation." For a criticism of the method of correlation I find congenial to my own, see Francis Schüssler Fiorenza, "Systematic Theology: Tasks and Methods," in *Systematic Theology: Roman Catholic Perspectives,* ed. Francis Schüssler Fiorenza and John P. Galvin (Minneapolis: Augsburg Fortress, 1991), 3–87.

11. George Lindbeck has argued persuasively that current trends in academic life are moving away from the kind of metaphysical inquiry Tracy urges and toward more modest "cultural-linguistic" forms of investigation. See *The Nature of Doctrine* (Philadelphia: Westminster Press, 1984), 15–29. Theologians should not adopt such methods simply because they represent the current academic trend, but it is interesting to note that today's intellectual climate within the university is more hospitable to an emphasis on particularity than at any time in the past two centuries.

12. Clifford Geertz, "Thick Description: Toward an Interpretive Theory of Culture," *The Interpretation of Cultures* (New York: Basic Books, 1973), 10.

13. Tracy, *Analogical Imagination,* 4.

14. See Chapter 7, "Piety, Narrative, and Christian Identity."

15. In this regard, I am in agreement with the argument offered by William Werpehowski in his important article "Ad Hoc Apologetics," *Journal of Religion* 66, no. 3 (July 1986): 282–301.

16. This account of theology's critical engagement with the forces of contemporary society should suffice to answer the serious charges made by James Gustafson against "purely descriptive theology." In his article "The Sectarian Temptation: Reflections on Theology, the Church, and the University," *Proceedings of the Catholic Theological Society* 40 (1985): 83–94, Gustafson asks whether "confessional" theologies can "provide a critical religious vision of reality that can aggressively interact with other ways of construing the world" (90). Gustafson proceeds to argue that "historic theologies, including Christian, if they are speaking about the ultimate power and orderer of life in the world, must be open to *revision and correction* in the face of alternative views" (93, italics added). In the ensuing controversy over Gustafson's use of the term "sectarian," this essential point about theology's openness to revision and correction has too often been overlooked. I hope that my account of a descriptive public theology responds, at least in principle, to Gustafson's concern. David Kelsey raises a similar point about George Lindbeck's theology in his recent article "Church Discourse and Public Realm," *Theology and Dialogue: Essays in Conversation With George Lindbeck* (Notre Dame: University of Notre Dame Press, 1990).

17. The best critical discussion of "postliberal" theology is to be found in William C. Placher, "Revisionist and Postliberal Theologies and the Public Char-

acter of Theology," *The Thomist* 49, no. 3 (July 1985): 392–416, and *Unapologetic Theology: A Christian Voice in a Pluralistic Conversation* (Louisville: Westminster/John Knox Press, 1989). My position is most closely related to the suggestions for future development of theology that Placher offers in the final chapter of his book. I am indebted to his remarkably clear and useful discussion of the major issues confronting contemporary theology.

18. Ronald F. Thiemann, *Revelation and Theology: The Gospel as Narrated Promise* (Notre Dame: University of Notre Dame Press, 1985), 74–75.

19. Perhaps a candid discussion of the differences among us will help to dispel the notion that there is a new "Yale School" in American theology. As those of us who have been identified as belonging in the "postliberal" camp engage in more constructive projects, our dissimilarities are likely to become more important and more interesting.

20. The best analysis of the relation between Christianity and political liberalism is William Werpehowski, "Political Liberalism and Christian Ethics: A Review Discussion," *The Thomist* 48, no. 1 (January 1984): 81–115. I believe that Hauerwas is too dependent on the analysis of liberalism provided by Alasdair MacIntyre in *After Virtue* (Notre Dame: University of Notre Dame Press, 1981) and *Whose Justice? Which Rationality?* (Notre Dame: University of Notre Dame Press, 1988). For an account of political liberalism that shows the inner connection between that tradition and a concern for religious freedom, see David A. J. Richards, *Toleration and the Constitution* (New York: Oxford University Press, 1986). In order to see the remarkable diversity that is possible within the liberal political tradition, see Nancy L. Rosenblum, *Liberalism and the Moral Life* (Cambridge: Harvard University Press, 1989). For my own extended analysis of the relation between Christian convictions and the liberal tradition, particularly on the question of pluralism in the public realm, see *Religion in American Public Life: A Dilemma for Democracy* (forthcoming).

21. I also find Lindbeck's emphasis on issues of text and textuality to be of limited assistance in the task of a public theology. In my response to his essay "Barth and Textuality," *Theology Today* 42, no. 3 (October 1986): 361–376, I express my worry that excessive attention to the question of *text* may deflect our attention from the more important issue of the relevance of talk of *God* in our secular culture. I also question whether the deconstructionalists' emphasis on "intratextuality" offers any assistance to the Christian effort to engage in public theology (377–382). I expand on this latter point in Chapter 2. For an insightful analysis of the limitations of Lindbeck's metaphors "language" and "culture" for conceiving of the church's relation to public life, see Kelsey, "Church Discourse and Public Realm." For a similar critique, see Rowan D. Williams, "Postmodern Theology and the Judgment of the World," in *Postmodern Theology: Christian Faith in a Pluralist World,* ed. Frederic B. Burnham (San Francisco: Harper & Row, 1989), 92–112.

22. It could be argued that the status of the church as a community of dissent, or a confessing church, might be best preserved within the polity of liberal democracy.

1

TOWARD AN AMERICAN
PUBLIC THEOLOGY:
RELIGION
IN A PLURALISTIC DEMOCRACY

In the years since the 1989 inauguration of George Bush as president of the United States, we have heard a good deal of talk about the restoration of American values, particularly those associated with the family and volunteer activity. In the intervening years, some political commentators have expressed scepticism about the president's rhetoric regarding values. They point out that during the 1988 presidential campaign, candidate Bush stressed the importance of American values while condoning a campaign strategy that appealed to some of the basest of American vices. Will the same contradiction between rhetoric and reality characterize the Bush presidency?

It has been pointed out that the 1988 presidential campaign was long on images and sound-bites but pitifully short on issues and substance. In some ways, the lack of substantive discussion during the presidential race was surprising, because it appeared at the outset of the primary campaigns that we were being presented with candidates who might force into the open some issues that had long lay dormant in American politics. The candidacies of Pat Robertson and Jesse Jackson in particular raised the expectation that we might at last engage in some serious national discussion about the role of religion in American public life. Many hoped that such consideration might then lead to substantive conversation about the values that are central to American democracy. Those hopes and expectations were dashed, however, in the postprimary campaign. Although both candidates referred to "values" throughout their campaigns, a close analysis of the texts of the remarks in the two presidential "debates" revealed that both candidates consistently failed to specify those values, preferring to use the word as an affective mechanism for evoking the "good feelings" of the American public.

This lost opportunity was particularly disappointing, given the fact that the presidential election occurred the year after we commemorated the bicentennial of the United States Constitution. The bicentennial observances, in contrast to the presidential campaign, evoked a good deal of reflection about the future of the American republic. Conferences, publications, and declarations sought to renew a sense of the vision incorporated in our nation's founding documents, a vision of freedom in the service of justice and the general welfare, a dream of individual initiative dedicated to the common good. The bicentennial of the Constitution gave us an opportunity to reflect on the fate of the founders' dream for America, and to see whether the dream has a future as we look toward the twenty-first century; yet that opportunity had little or no impact upon presidential politics.

The lack of serious attention to the question of national values is especially distressing, because the American people seem to be experiencing a crisis of confidence about our public life. Insider trading on Wall Street, widespread corruption within the business community, a consistent pattern of dishonesty and deception within government, the fraudulent practices of television evangelists, the apparent lack of public interest among upwardly mobile professionals: these are just some of the concerns that led *Time* magazine recently to ask on its cover, "What Ever Happened to Ethics?" At a more profound level, the much discussed book *Habits of the Heart* has raised the specter of a "cancerous" new individualism that "may be threatening the survival of freedom itself."[1]

This malaise within our public life appears so widespread and pervasive that it raises basic questions about the moral fabric of our society. Are we as a nation and a people committed to values that uphold some sense of the common good? Do we share any basic convictions or values, or have we become so diverse that our deepest beliefs are simply a matter of personal preference and individual self-interest? These questions are being raised precisely at a time when religion has emerged as a significant force in American politics.

During the 1980s, we witnessed the rise of an aggressive new form of evangelical Christian politics, a development that has raised a whole range of questions about the role of religion in American public life. Does the emergence of a self-consciously Christian politics threaten the freedom of those religious, ethnic, and cultural minorities who have gained precious civil rights since the end of the Second World War? Does the presence of religious rhetoric in the public arena pose a threat to that so-called wall of separation between church and state established by the First Amendment? Are the interests of the American people best served by a benign and neutral secular republic or by a republic that actively encourages the equal flourishing of all religions?

These questions about public religion are being raised precisely at this time of crisis in our public life. In this chapter I want to explore the inner connections between these two issues: the relation between public religion and public values.

THE PROPER PUBLIC ROLE OF RELIGION

The question of the proper role of religion and of religiously based moral convictions within American public life was, of course, a hotly debated topic during the 1980s. Despite the growing recognition that religion inevitably plays a crucial role in forming and shaping public values, some commentators still argue that religion should be denied a public role in a pluralistic democracy in which the separation of church and state is constitutionally required. Others, acknowledging the inevitable role of religion in public affairs, have sought to identify an appropriate but limited place for religion or religiously based moral convictions. It is fair to say that there is today no genuine consensus among the American people concerning the public role of religion.

The contention that religion ought to play no public role in American life is a peculiar late-twentieth-century position. It would hardly have been disputed during most of American history that religious convictions were and ought to be among the most important convictions governing the formulation of public policy. The rhetoric of the American republic has always been religious: the justification for the American Revolution was developed from the conviction that "all men are created equal, that they are endowed by their *Creator* with certain unalienable rights"; in the Pledge of Allegiance that most public school children still recite every morning, we describe ourselves as "one nation under God." American presidents have been among our most important public theologians, interpreting our history in theological categories, invoking the judgment of God over the actions of the American people. The master of the art of public theology was Abraham Lincoln, as a brief excerpt from his Second Inaugural Address will testify.

> If we shall suppose that American slavery is one of those offenses which, in the providence of God, must needs come, but which, having continued through His appointed time, He now wills to remove, and

that He gives to both North and South this terrible war as the woe due to those by whom the offense came, shall we discern therein any departure from those divine attributes which the believers in a living God always ascribe to Him? Fondly do we hope, fervently do we pray, that this mighty scourge of war may speedily pass away. Yet, if God wills that it continue until all the wealth piled by the bondsman's two hundred and fifty years of unrequited toil shall be sunk, and until every drop of blood drawn with the lash shall be paid by another drawn with the sword, as was said three thousand years ago, so still it must be said "the judgments of the Lord are true and righteous altogether."[2]

Not only are these sentences rhetorically more sophisticated than most political discourse we are likely to hear today, but they offer a robust and straightforward theological interpretation of the events of the Civil War. It is hard to imagine such rhetoric emerging from the mouth of a contemporary politician. Lincoln's theological discourse would hardly play in a culture in which religious and moral convictions are thought to be merely private and in which invocations of the deity are reduced to former President Reagan's benign and clichéd "God bless" at the end of every speech. And yet it was less than thirty years ago that John F. Kennedy could summon up resonances of both Jefferson and Lincoln in his inaugural address.

For I have sworn before you and Almighty God the same solemn oath our forebears prescribed nearly a century and three quarters ago. The world is very different now. For we hold in our mortal hands the power to abolish all forms of human poverty and to abolish all forms of human life. And yet the same revolutionary beliefs for which our forebears fought are still at issue around the globe—the belief that the rights of man come not from the generosity of the state but from the hand of God.[3]

Yet despite the apparent religious content of this address, a contemporary theologian, writing just four years after the Kennedy inaugural, pointed to Kennedy's pragmatic political style as a key example of ethos of "the secular city."[4] The rhetoric may have been religious, but the style and substance of America's first Roman Catholic president was not in any evident way motivated by religious convictions.

RELIGION'S RHETORICAL POWER AND POLITICAL IMPOTENCE

That contrast between religious rhetoric and political reality points to an important tension that has characterized the American republic since its founding. The philosophical defense of the American experiment in democracy has almost always been formulated in religious categories. The Declaration of Independence is rife with religious presuppositions and assertions; the rhetoric of our public figures as they seek to summon the support of the American people for the preservation of the Union, or the search for the New Frontier, or the building of the Great Society, or the defense of civil rights has often been couched in religious and even biblical cadences. It is important to remember, of course, that the same biblical language has also been used to justify the Spanish-American War, the annexation of the Philippines, and the inexorable westward expansion that resulted in the slaughter of many Native Americans and the displacement of the rest.

But precisely as this theological and biblical justification for American policy was being developed, we devised and refined a governing mechanism that was rigorously secular in its operation. The United States Constitution can hardly be mistaken for a religious document. Indeed, one of its most important provisions is the strict separation of church and state, of the political and the religious, in the governance of the American democracy. This constitutional separation prevents the establishment of any religion as the American state church and guarantees the free expression of religious (or nonreligious) practice in all its diversity. Moreover, it presupposes a plurality of competing interests among the American people. The Federalist papers envision a populace motivated by "ambition, avarice, personal animosity, [and] party opposition," and the authors urge the development of a government in which such interests are balanced against one another, thus curbing that "torrent of angry and malignant passions" that would otherwise "be let loose."[5] Such a government must be neutral with regard to all interests, principles, and motivations, having as its only goal the equitable and just mediation of those competing interests and passions. Justice in such a system is genuinely blind to all principles and convictions, and seeks simply to provide equal access and equal opportunity for all individuals to pursue their private interests. If the government should ever represent or seek to grant advantage to some particular religious interest or conviction, it would by definition become unjust. Religion in the American republic is thus manifested as "public rhetoric and private virtue." As Peter Berger has written, "Insofar as religion is common it lacks 'reality', and insofar as it is 'real' its lacks commonality."[6]

That odd dichotomy between religion's rhetorical power and its political impotence has characterized much of our nation's history. Yet even at the time of the founding of the Republic, the authors of the Constitution recognized the need for some kind of public virtue. James Madison, in Federalist 45, argued that "public good, the real welfare of the great body of the people, is the supreme object to be pursued; and that no form of government whatever has any other value than as it may be fitted for the attainment of this object."[7] "Is there no virtue among us?" asked Madison. "If there be not, no form of government can render us secure. To suppose that any form of government will secure liberty or happiness without virtue in the people is a chimerical idea."[8] American constitutional democracy presupposes a virtuous public life, and yet it provides no positive encouragement for the development of such public virtue. Where then are the sources of such public virtue to be found? And how in the midst of our cultural, political, and moral pluralism are we to reach agreement concerning those values that should guide our public life?

CULTURAL PLURALISM

The framers of the Constitution did not have a very positive assessment of cultural pluralism. They tended to identify cultural differences with "factions," that is, groups of citizens motivated by self-interest, seeking their own good over that of the commonweal. Madison, in Federalist 10, writes: "The latent causes of faction are . . . sown in the nature of man. . . . [H]uman passions have . . . divided mankind into parties, inflamed them with mutual animosity, and rendered them much more disposed to vex and oppress each other than to cooperate for their common good."[9]

Despite this initial distrust of cultural pluralism, however, the American republic has exemplified a greater ethnic and cultural diversity than has any other modern nation. Successive generations of immigrants arrived on these shores and became "Americans" even as they maintained their ethnic identities. This process of "Americanization" often involved enormous struggle against profound prejudice, but one ethnic group after another has made the successful transition to full citizenship in their adopted land. The American dream has been profoundly transformed through this process, becoming far more inclusive than the framers of the Constitution could have imagined.

One of the greatest accomplishments of Dr. Martin Luther King Jr. can be seen in the way he used the rhetoric of the founding documents to overcome the racism inherent in those very documents. The Preamble of the Constitution asserted the framers' intention to "secure the blessings of liberty to ourselves and our posterity," whereas Article I defined slaves as three-fifths of a free person, insured the continuation of the slave trade at least until 1808, and allowed a tax on imported property not to exceed ten dollars per slave. And yet Dr. King, sitting in a Birmingham jail cell in 1963, could write: "We will reach the goal of freedom in Birmingham and all over the nation, because the goal of America is freedom. . . . We will win our freedom because the sacred heritage of our nation and the eternal will of God are embodied in our echoing demands."[10]

Ethnic and cultural pluralism has been a force for enormous good in the history of the American republic. Our national political debate has been greatly enriched by the lively positions and arguments put forward by women, African Americans, Hispanics, Native Americans, and others who had been previously excluded from political power and influence. Advances in the areas of civil and economic rights would have been inconceivable without the feisty pressures of such diverse groups. The American constitutional system has demonstrated its resilience by including these competing parties within the political process without rupturing those tender bonds that hold the nation together. But of just as much importance, these groups have helped to broaden the purview of the American dream by encouraging the development of those virtues of citizenship designed to serve the common good. The equation of such citizen groups with "self-interested factions" fails to recognize the enormous moral contributions these diverse people have made to our common public life.

And yet there is another form of pluralism that *is* having a corrosive effect upon our public life. Madison's worry about factions in American life was not entirely misplaced, for when political interests are disconnected from the virtues of citizenship, then that "torrent of angry and malignant passions" is indeed "let loose." When an interest group pursues its political aims without reference to the common good, then those values that bind us together as a nation are ultimately undermined. During the last decade, we have witnessed increasingly strident debates about issues of public policy. The fabric of our common national life has come under increasing pressure and may not long withstand opposing tugs of competing interest groups. Even more distressing is the fact that we seem to be losing our ability to engage in common discourse about the important political and moral issues facing the Republic. Is nuclear energy the "hopeful solution" or the "menacing threat" to a globe with diminishing fossil fuels and a depleted ozone layer? Is that which the pregnant woman carries a "fetus" or an "unborn child"? Our inability to reach linguistic consensus on such matters indicates that a deep moral pluralism underlies our current public debates.

There are those among us who despair of the possibility of any consensus on questions of value or public virtue. Alasdair MacIntyre, in his important book *After Virtue,* has argued that people who engage in ethical disputes about abortion or nuclear disarmament or homosexuality cannot reach agreement because they argue from "rival and incommensurable moral premises."[11] Moral disagreement, he asserts, is not simply an accidental result of a faulty process of adjudication; it is inherent in the very nature of contemporary moral disputes. Such disputes necessarily resist all efforts at adjudication. We have, he says, entered a new dark age; indeed, the barbarians are already governing us. And so we must retreat to our local communities, cultivate our local virtues, and await the coming of a new St. Benedict who might lead the way for virtue once again to appear on the public scene. But for now we must forgo public ethical activity and seek simply to preserve those few precious values that endure within communities separated from the public world.

MacIntyre's position is persuasively argued, and it has had a powerful impact, particularly among contemporary Christian ethicists. No one on the current intellectual scene has so clearly identified the moral dilemma of our contemporary public life, but in my judgment, MacIntyre's solution to that problem threatens us with even greater damage. If the virtues and values crucial to our common human life are being maintained within local communities, including communities of faith, then for that very reason we are under obligation to enter the public debate, using those moral resources, not to dominate, but to contribute to those conversations that will determine the policies that will shape our common human future.

THE CHALLENGE OF DEBATE

If we do enter that conversation, we must be prepared for a difficult and challenging debate. There are profound moral disagreements among those who contribute to the ongoing discussion concerning public policy. Let me give just a single example of the intractability of those disagreements.

Early in 1984, the Department of Health and Human Services adopted new guidelines for the treatment of severely handicapped newborns. The federal government developed those guidelines following the famous "Baby Doe" case in which an infant born with Down's syndrome and a digestive system blockage was allowed to die, in accordance with the parents' wishes, without receiving corrective surgery. Following that incident, the government issued controversial regulations requiring hospitals to give the same life-preserving care to handicapped infants as they would to the nonhandicapped. These regulations raise important issues about government intervention in private familial decisions and about the appropriate limits for extraordinary or heroic care, issues that still remain unresolved in the present public debate.

I will not offer here my own assessment of those issues.[12] Rather, I want to describe one important contribution to the discussion made by Peter Singer and Helga Kuhse in an article they wrote for the *New York Times Book Review* in March 1984. I do so because their argument illustrates how deeply divided our society is regarding the most basic moral assumptions. Singer and Kuhse do not raise the standard objections about governmental intervention or heroic care. They rather oppose the underlying principle that they suggest motivated the government's position, namely, the belief that "all human lives are of equal worth." The authors state their conclusions straightforwardly: "We cannot coherently hold that it is all right to kill a fetus a week before birth, but as soon as the baby is born everything must be done to keep it alive. The solution, however, is not to accept the pro-life view that the fetus is a human being with the same moral status as yours or mine. The solution is the very opposite: to abandon the idea that all human life is of equal worth."

I want to make it very clear how I am using this example. I am not seeking to evaluate the persuasiveness of the so-called pro-life or pro-choice positions. I am rather seeking to show how certain kinds of arguments, grounded in particular premises, can challenge values that are often thought to be central to the public morality that underlies our democratic society. The principle of "equal regard" has played an indispensable role in the quest for justice in the United States. It has been invoked in the fight against slavery, in the struggle for women's suffrage, in the civil rights movement, and in efforts for ratification of the Equal Rights Amendment. Singer and Kuhse oppose not just a particular application of this principle; they oppose the principle itself. And their rationale is extremely important, precisely for the question of the degree to which religious beliefs ought to influence public policy decisions. The authors argue that the belief in the equal worth of all human life is a particular Christian conviction that is not shared by all participants in American public life. To organize federal guidelines around a specific religious belief is to introduce "a special brand of ideological or religious zeal" into the public sphere. The principle of "equal regard," Singer and Kuhse argue, is not a belief that expresses the consensus of American citizens but a particular Christian doctrine masquerading as a commonly held national conviction.

The deep moral pluralism of our culture challenges the very notion that there can be a fundamental value orientation that binds a people together in common action within the public realm. At the same time, to reject the idea that we share any common human values or virtues is to strike at the very heart of the notion of political community. We must find a way between the cultural and religious imperialism that would define the interests and values of one group as the common good, and the moral relativism that would assert that all values and ethical stances are nothing more than the opinions or personal preferences of those who hold them. The former position is a denial of pluralism, the latter a denial that we can share anything in common even as we acknowledge our differences. The former position allows the tyrannical suppression of minorities and dissent; the latter position allows the politics of interest to overwhelm the fragile but important vision of a public-spirited citizenry. The great challenge to American democracy today is to find a way between these equally unhappy alternatives.

WHAT MORE CAN THE CHURCH DO?

In the final sections of this chapter, I want to raise the question of whether Christian churches can once again play a role in nurturing those "habits of the heart" that might help us seek after a common human future. I want to inquire whether Christian theology can do more than provide the ideological rhetoric for political programs—whether it can once again play a role in forming the reality out of which American public policy might be formed.

It is clear that the return of religion to the public arena is fraught with dangers. Insofar as religion has provided some common focus for American public life throughout our history, it has done so primarily under the banner of a broadly Christian "civil religion." Whatever common religion we have shared in the past has been a form of Protestant Christianity. That common religion was formed in the crucible of early Puritan culture and dominated American life through the nineteenth century. In the early 1800s, Supreme Court Justice Joseph Story asserted that "there will probably be found few persons in this, or any other Christian country, who would deliberately contend that it was unreasonable or unjust to foster and encourage the Christian religion generally, as a matter of sound policy, as well as of revealed truth."[13] Philip Schaff, a distinguished church historian of the late nineteenth century, argued that "Christianity is the most powerful factor in our society and the pillar of our institutions. . . . Christianity is the only possible religion for the American people, and with Christianity are bound up all our hopes for the future."[14]

Whether such judgments were in fact true even in the nineteenth century, they certainly were *believed* to be true by a large majority of Americans. Such judgments, though they are still uttered by some Americans today, are no longer believed to be true by most citizens. It is surely the case that even if some form of common American religion existed through the nineteenth century, it most assuredly does not exist today. The United States is a religiously plural country, counting within its diversity not only a wide variety of Christian denominations and various forms of Judaism, but increasing numbers of Islamic, Buddhist, and other Asian religious communities, as well as millions of persons who do not identify themselves as traditionally religious. Any attempt to revive a role for religion within the public sphere must recognize the religious pluralism of American culture.

If our common American religion no longer exists, then how can American religious communities make a contribution toward some common good for America? Obviously, I cannot provide anything like a definitive answer to that question within the scope of this chapter, but I would like to make a few points that might indicate the way toward the future of this discussion.

First, religious pluralism can be an important resource in the search for a new common good for America. Christianity, and particularly Protestant Christianity, has exercised enormous influence over our cultural and political life—for both good and ill. Christianity's influence has been most devastating when its moral and religious fervor has been linked to unchecked political power. Genuine religious pluralism means that Christians must recognize themselves as one religious voice among others in the public conversation. Surely, Christianity will continue to be a major religious force in American life well into the twenty-first century, but we must debunk the myth that we are a "Christian nation," and we must restrain those forces that seek to impose some form of Christian politics on American public life. Christians should seek to preserve a genuinely plural and diverse conversation in the public sphere.

Second, we must also debunk the myth that religion has no role in American public life. The constitutional separation of church and state prevents the *establishment* of any religion as the American state church and guarantees the free expression of religious (or nonreligious) practice in all its diversity. That constitutional safeguard does not, however, imply that questions of conviction, value, and faith are to be forbidden from public discourse. Indeed, such things have never been absent. The recent prominence of the religious right in American politics has continued a long tradition of religious discourse in the political realm—a tradition practiced with great skill by some of our presidents. The problem with the political voice of the religious right is not that it is religious but that it has too often been exclusive and intolerant of those who do not share Christian values.

Third, the rise of the religious right has corresponded to the gradual decline of liberal Christianity and, to some extent, liberal Judaism. The liberal strategy of accommodation to the reigning culture, precisely at the time when that culture has become success and achievement oriented, is a strategy that guarantees the continuing public impotence of the Christian tradition. I am convinced that religious communities will recover their public voices only when they rediscover their own roots, only when they seek to appropriate and reform their own religious traditions. Recovery of an authentic public voice and rediscovery of religious heritage must go hand in hand.

It is with regard to this issue that I believe American Protestantism stands at a significant crossroads in its history. The disestablishment of the "old line" Protestant churches as a major cultural force in the United States has created a new situation within American public life. The most important contributions to contemporary public affairs in recent decades have come not from the liberal Protestant tradition but from those religious communities that have maintained relatively coherent religious identities—the historic black churches and post–Vatican II Roman Catholicism. For all the internal disputes within these communities, they continue to live out of a tradition that provides a coherent context for conversation and debate. When communities lose touch with their own traditions, they also undermine their ability to participate in and influence the public discussion. Communities that are undergoing a perpetual identity crisis do not make for interesting conversation partners. American Protestant churches will not recover their public voices until they seek to recover and reform their own religious traditions.

Fourth, ours is a highly politicized era, and many, both within and without the church, seek their salvation through political activity. Surrogate gospels often emerge in the guise of political ideologies, some neoconservative, some liberal, some Marxist or radical. Each of those political ideologies offers a program for public life worth examining, but none of them offers a ready-made solution for Christian involvement in public affairs. The story of liberal Protestant involvement in American public life since the 1930s has been the increasingly uninteresting tale of the alliance between mainstream Protestants and the liberal wing of the Democratic party. That has been an important and influential alliance (and my personal political beliefs incline me to support many of the policies developed through that alliance); but since the Vietnam era, political liberalism has been in a state of disarray, and mainstream Protestants have gone looking for a new partner. Some have wandered into the neoconservative camp and have sought to create a new covenant between Christianity and democratic capitalism. Others have looked toward movements of liberation to provide orientation for Christian public involvement.

But no simple alliance will do. There is no single solution to the problem of the relation between the church and public life. The church cannot escape the inevitable ambiguity of the concreteness of its own life and that of its nation. Given the complexity of contemporary social, political, and ethical issues, the church can no longer be content to focus its public ministry primarily on the issuance of social statements and public proclamations. The confusion in our public life is sufficiently acute that we need to devise new models for the development of public policies. The decades-long privatization of religion has brought about an unhealthy separation of the public policy disciplines from the deepest sources of human faith, conviction, and hope. The quantification of the social sciences has introduced a sharp distinction between questions of fact and value, between the descriptive and normative aspects of decision making. The policymakers who graduate from places like Harvard's business school or its Kennedy School of Government are among the most highly skilled economists and strategic planners in the world, but they are woefully lacking in sophistication about the moral uses and limits of the power their education has granted them. At the same time, the graduates of our seminaries and divinity schools are woefully lacking in sophistication about the empirical studies so crucial to contemporary policy formation.

Our society desperately needs people who will bring a commitment to justice into the public sphere, people who have both the intelligence and the patience to bring together a vision of righteousness with the careful analysis of public policy. We have enough prophets who fire their moral broadsides against the evils of our society; we have enough policymakers who determine our future through efficiency studies and cost-effective analyses. What we lack are those who combine prophetic vision with careful analysis; and until we cultivate and nurture such persons, our public life will remain diffuse and spiritless.

In order for such a meeting of faith and empirical science to occur, the churches must give attention to new forms of education. We must seek to create forums within which genuine debate and dialogue about crucial public issues can take place. The last decade has seen the rise of many institutes, centers, and "think tanks" devoted to advocating some particular cause or interest. These advocacy centers function primarily to encourage the "politics of interest" rather than the "politics of the common good." And because they are well funded, they tend to advocate the interests of the rich and powerful. What we lack is a concerted educational effort to link theological training with empirically grounded policy studies. If such an initiative is to be launched, it will require a large-scale effort by many different kinds of institutions. I believe that the churches have a distinctive role to play in this effort, for we have in our midst numerous persons who combine a commitment of faith with sophistication in policy fields, namely, our laity. But we need to think creatively about ways to provide the ethical and theological training these public leaders will need, even as we seek to devise programs to introduce seminarians, pastors, and church leaders to the public policy dimensions of their ministries.

Fifth, one of the most encouraging developments in the sphere of public affairs in recent years has been the American bishops' pastorals on peace and economic justice. Those statements have been both praised and criticized, but they have made the important contribution of introducing overt theological discourse and analysis into the public debate. Their positions have received widespread media coverage and have elicited thoughtful responses from scholars and policymakers outside the religious community. The question remains whether their statements will have any real or lasting impact on the structure of public policy—whether they will move beyond rhetoric to influence our common public reality.

There has been a great deal of discussion in academic theology about "public theology." Most of that debate has focused on the question of whether theological arguments are available for public examination and whether theological assertions are intelligible beyond the confines of a particular religious community. Although such issues are intellectually interesting and important within a rather small circle of academic theologians, they only begin to help us address what I consider far more important questions: Will religious convictions and theological analyses have any real impact on the way our public lives are structured? Can a truly public theology have a salutary influence on the development of public policy within a pluralistic democratic nation? The real challenge to a North American public theology is to find a way— within the social, cultural, and religious pluralism of North American politics—to influence the development of public policy without seeking to construct a new Christendom or lapsing into a benign moral relativism.

The rampant rise of individualism within our culture threatens to create a radical imbalance between self-interest and common interest, between private gain and public good. A society in which individual success and achievement are valued above all else is a society in which the gap between the successful and the failed, between those who achieve and those who do not, between the rich and the poor can only widen. It is important for us to ask where the countervailing values of communal commitment, of care for the poor and abandoned, of concern for those human values we share in common no matter what our status or degree of success—where those virtues can be nourished. Clearly, such virtues continue to be present in our public life, but my concern is that the institutions that have traditionally nourished them are increasingly committed to the culture of individualism and egoism. Churches and synagogues have in the past helped to foster those "habits of the heart" that allowed for the development of a civic-minded, public-spirited citizenry. We can do so again if we develop a new vision of how excellence and compassion, self-interest and virtue, private gain and public good can once again be brought together. If churches can once again become "schools of public virtue," communities that seek to form the kind of character necessary for public life, then they can play an essential role in helping to forge a more compassionate but no less excellent vision of the American dream.

NOTES

1. Robert N. Bellah, Richard Madsen, William M. Sullivan, Ann Swidler, and Steven M. Tipton, *Habits of the Heart* (Berkeley: University of California Press, 1985), viii.

2. As quoted in *American Historical Documents,* ed. Harold C. Syrett (New York: Barnes & Noble, 1960), 283.

3. John F. Kennedy, *Public Papers of the Presidents of the United States: Containing the Public Messages, Speeches, and Statements of the President* (Washington, D.C.: U.S. Government Printing Office WOC 1962).

4. Harvey Cox, *The Secular City* (New York: Macmillan, 1965).

5. James Madison et al., *The Federalist Papers,* ed. Clinton Rossiter (New York: New American Library, 1961), 79.

6. Peter Berger, *The Sacred Canopy* (Garden City, N.Y.: Doubleday, 1968), 134.

7. Madison, *The Federalist Papers,* 289.

8. Madison is cited as having said these words at the Virginia ratification convention. See Jonathon Elliott, *The Debates in Several State Conventions on the Adoption of the Federal Constitution,* vol. 3 (Philadelphia: J. B. Lippincott & Co., 1836), 536–537.

9. Madison, *The Federalist Papers,* 79.

10. Martin Luther King Jr., "Letter from a Birmingham City Jail," in *A Testament of Hope: The Essential Writings of Martin Luther King, Jr.,* ed. James M. Washington (San Francisco: Harper & Row, 1986), 301.

11. Alasdair MacIntyre, *After Virtue* (Notre Dame: University of Notre Dame Press, 1981), 6–21.

12. I will treat these issues in much greater detail in my forthcoming book, *Religion in American Public Life: A Dilemma for Democracy.*

13. Joseph Story, *Commentaries on the Constitution of the United States,* vol. 2 (Boston: Gray Hilliard, 1833), 723. Quoted by John Wilson, "Common Religion in American Society," in *Civil Religion and Political Theology,* ed. Leroy Rouner (Notre Dame: University of Notre Dame Press, 1986), 113–114.

14. Philip Schaff, "Church and State in the United States," in *Papers of the American Historical Association,* vol. 2, no. 4 (New York, 1888). Quoted by John Wilson, "Common Religion in American Society," 114.

2

RADIANCE AND OBSCURITY IN
BIBLICAL NARRATIVES

In Kafka's *The Trial,* a priest recounts a tale about a man seeking entrance to the law. The door to the law is guarded by a series of terrible doorkeepers determined to turn away all who would seek entrance. The man, undeterred by these obstacles, resolves to wait, and so sits on his stool, cajoling, even bribing, the doorkeeper, but to no avail. Finally, after many years of waiting, the man begins to slip into death. In his final moments, he notes a beautiful light streaming from the door and seeks from the doorkeeper some explanation for these strange occurrences. The doorkeeper replies, "This door was intended only for you. Now I am going to shut it." With that the parable ends.[1]

THE PATH OF INTERPRETATION

Frank Kermode has made a great deal of Kafka's story, using it in his book *The Genesis of Secrecy* to argue that all interpreters of narratives are finally outsiders, readers who seek to discover a tale's radiant mystery but always fail. Our efforts to understand run up against "an uninterpretable radiance," so they die, like the seeker of the law, frustrated and unfulfilled. "All narratives are essentially dark," Kermode argues, and the worlds that they cast up before us are finally "unfollowable." "World and book," Kermode writes, "are hopelessly plural, endlessly disappointing. . . . [O]ur sole hope and pleasure is in the perception of a momentary radiance, before the door of disappointment is finally shut on us."[2]

Kermode states with particular eloquence what has become a commonplace of contemporary hermeneutics—that literary texts are indeterminable and thus inevitably yield multiple, irreducibly diverse interpretations. Some theorists have readily drawn a further conclusion, one that does not necessarily follow from the fact of multiple interpretations; namely, that there can be no criteria for preferring one reading to another and that we are therefore cast into the darkest of hermeneutical nights in which all readings are indistinguishably gray. Such hermeneutical relativism surely does suggest that both text and world are hopelessly unfollowable, that the brief glimmer of light emitted by shadowy narratives is hardly sufficient to light the path of interpretation, much less to illumine an entire world of experience. And so we are left to stumble about in the dark, making our way as best we can.

This view of interpretation and of the human condition has been powerfully and persuasively presented by contemporary literary critics. Many critics, the deconstructionists chief among them, recognize the important political implications of their hermeneutical arguments. By loosing interpretation from the authoritative grasp of "the metaphysics of presence," they hope to revive the freedom necessary for a critical humanism.[3] The world created by Christendom, ruled by the Christian God, and governed by the philosophers of being must fall if freedom, difference, and playfulness are to flourish.

The hermeneutical position represented by Kermode and others has become so persuasive in part because we have so many confirming experiences of relativism within our own cultural situation. American public life exhibits many of the vices and virtues of our current cultural pluralism. As I argued in the previous chapter, our national culture has profitted enormously from the ethnic, cultural, and political diversity that characterizes our society. Such pluralism need not lead to cultural relativism, as long as these various groups share some common goals and aspirations. It is becoming increasingly evident, however, that our healthy pluralist tradition is showing signs of severe strain and deepening fissures.

Even more distressing is the fact that we seem to be losing our ability to engage in common discourse about the important political and moral issues facing the Republic. The debates concerning abortion provide the most evident and painful example of the collapse of any apparent consensus on the most basic ethical questions. Do we call that which the woman carries a fetus or an unborn child? Do we call the act of abortion the termination of a pregnancy or the taking of innocent life? Our failure to reach even linguistic consensus on these matters indicates that a deep moral pluralism underlies the current debate about abortion.

Such moral pluralism can then too easily connote not just a fruitful diversity of opinion but the belief that such diversity is irreducible, that is, that there can be no rational procedures for adjudicating not only conflicting interpretations of texts but for adjudicating those deep moral and political disagreements within our culture. This new pluralism will be sustained by the conviction that opposing positions regarding abortion or nuclear disarmament or social welfare programs are simply equally unjustifiable opinions that express the personal preferences of those who hold them. There are no reasons or arguments that can ultimately decide such matters, and thus they must be decided simply by the exercise of power (a position clearly illustrated by the recent tragic bombings of abortion clinics).

To believe that ethical positions are nothing more than expressions of personal preferences or cultural differences, to believe that our deepest beliefs and convictions are simply nonrational opinions, is to despair of the possibility of any significant common life within the Republic. People who hold these beliefs have no motivation to participate in the common good of the nation. They have no reason to listen to the arguments of those with whom they disagree. And finally, they have no reason to curb their own excesses in defending those positions that most accord with their own personal preferences—no matter how harmful those positions may be to the community as a whole.

Political and cultural diversity is a gift to be nurtured and celebrated. The freedom upon which such diversity is based is particularly precious and must be preserved and extended to those who have been excluded from full participation in a free society. But like all gifts of God's creation, these blessings have been touched by the distorting power of sin. Freedom yoked to selfishness becomes avarice, and diversity contemptuous of the common good yields a nation of isolated individuals.

The consequences of unbridled pluralism are not as evident in hermeneutics as they are in political life, but, as the avant garde critics rightly remind us, the interpretive positions we adopt in the academy ultimately have political implications. Too often, however, these critics assume that their deconstruction of text and world is an occasion for pure celebration. But there is another darker side to their exuberant subversion of the tradition that has sought to use texts to enlighten a world, a side seen clearly by one of the fathers of deconstruction, Friedrich Nietzsche.

In that famous scene from "The Gay Science," a madman runs into a crowded marketplace crying, "I seek God! I seek God!" As the crowd taunts and ridicules him, the madman jumps into their midst and pierce[s] them with his glances. "Whither is God," he cried. "I shall tell you. WE HAVE KILLED HIM—you and I. All of us are his murderers. But how have we done this? Who gave us the sponge to wipe away the entire horizon? What did we do when we unchained this earth from its horizon? Whither is it moving now? Whither are we moving now? Away from all suns? Are we not plunging continually? . . . God is dead. God remains dead. And we have killed him. How shall we, the murderers of all murderers, comfort ourselves? . . . Is not the greatness of this deed too great for us? Must not we ourselves become gods simply to seem worthy of it?"[4]

Nietzsche recognized clearly that the end of the authoritative tradition that Christianity had spawned and nurtured meant not only a bracing new freedom but a profound sense of intellectual and ethical vertigo. A world without a horizon is a world without balance. A world without illumination is a world plunging away from all suns into cold and darkness. The only way to regain our balance in such a disorienting situation is for us to become gods ourselves.

It is important to remember that Frank Kermode grounds his case about "narrative obscurity" through an analysis of the Gospel of Mark. Thus he raises his hermeneutical challenge to textual enlightenment by deconstructing one of the texts that for almost two millennia has been central to the self-understanding of the Christian community and through that community to much of Western culture. The Gospel narratives continue to be the central formative texts of Christianity, whatever their more uncertain fate within our broader culture. Consequently, the claim that narrative texts can depict and illumine a followable world is one that Christians are concerned to defend, not as a general principle, but as a proposition that is true with reference to the Bible. Yet Christians must take care to define clearly the claims they wish to defend, or they might find themselves committed to positions that are ultimately indefensible.

EXAMINING THE BIBLICAL NARRATIVES

I intend to argue that biblical narratives *do* illumine a followable world for the readers of those texts. But before I launch into a more detailed account of that argument, I want to engage in a little deconstruction of my own by attempting to subvert an erroneous assumption that has haunted the current hermeneutical discussion.

Many philosophers and literary critics (including Nietzsche, Kermode, and some of the deconstructionists) have assumed that texts must either be perspicacious or totally indeterminate. Kermode, for example, sets up the contrast between "insiders" and "outsiders," between "spiritual" and "carnal" readings, between pellucid and obscure narratives in order to show that inside and spiritual interpretations are finally illusory. They can be powerful illusions, particularly when buttressed by the authority of institutions, but they are for all their influence illusions nonetheless. We are all finally outsiders. Thus Kermode does not really transcend his own dichotomy but finally absorbs one term of his contrasting pair into the other. So also Nietzsche, at least in "The Gay Science," poses the alternatives of a stable God-oriented world or dizzy free-fall into the darkness. Finally, Derrida and his followers appear to offer a similar dichotomy in their contrast between the presence and centeredness of the onto-theological tradition and their own focus on absence and difference. In every case, these thinkers seem to be victims of what Richard Bernstein has called "the Cartesian anxiety"—that "grand and seductive Either/Or. *Either* there is some support for our being, a fixed foundation for our knowledge, *or* we cannot escape the forces of darkness that envelop us with madness, with intellectual and moral chaos."[5] With varying degrees of fervor, these postmodern thinkers are urging us to come to terms with the madness and chaos that is our inevitable fate.

But madness is inevitable only if illumination is unachievable. And illumination is unachievable only if it is construed as a perfect light that dispels all darkness and banishes all shadows. Admittedly, modern philosophers and theologians have often seen their task as one of seeking the ultimate source of knowledge that enlightens all understanding. The eighteenth-century philosophes called their movement "enlightenment" because they were confident that reason was the beacon that would lead them into all truth. Modern theologians have relied heavily upon images of light and vision in order to express God's illuminating self-disclosure in revelation. In each case, these philosophers and theologians have conceived the goal of inquiry to be the discovery of an unshakable, incorrigible foundation for knowledge. The true foundation for knowledge needs no external illumination but glows with the light of self-illumination. Only such a *sui generis* source of enlightenment can serve as the basis for human assurance and security.[7]

As the contemporary philosophical discussion has shown, this epistemological foundationalism is conceptually incoherent.[8] Ironically, the deconstructionists, who have been among the most vigorous critics of this foundational tradition, remain wedded to the essential assumptions of that tradition when they seek to describe the consequences of their own criticism. Madness, darkness, and chaos follow inevitably only if there is no other alternative to perfect illumination. In rejecting the "either" of Descartes' search for clarity and distinctness, they seize the "or" of Cartesian anxiety. Kermode, for example, seems to assume that because literary texts yield multiple interpretations they are therefore "endlessly disappointing" and "unfollowable." Interpretive diversity does not necessarily imply hermeneutical relativism. Nor does the fact of such diversity decide the question of whether texts yield followable worlds.

In arguing that biblical narratives illumine a followable world, I am not denying that there are other plausible readings of these narratives, including readings that stress primarily the obscurity and indeterminacy of these texts. The fact that multiple interpretations of biblical narratives are possible does not decide the issue of whether any one interpretation is more plausible than any other. Nor does the phenomenon of "narrative obscurity" preclude the existence of criteria by which we can decide upon preferable readings. What interpretive diversity does determine is that such questions cannot be settled abstractly or theoretically, that is, in isolation from actual interpretations of the text. Only when we look at detailed rival readings of a narrative can we be in a position to judge between them. Whether a narrative portrays a followable world cannot be decided on the basis of one's theory of narrativity. Interpreters must risk interpretations, and readers must patiently hear and evaluate their exegesis before deciding whether a plausible world has been presented and whether such a world is inhabitable. "Followability," is a predicate of particular narratives, not of one's theory about all possible narratives.

Erich Auerbach, in his monumental study of realism in Western literature, noted two qualities of biblical and particularly Hebrew biblical narrative. Such stories are "mysterious and 'fraught with background' ";[9] they heighten suspense by describing terrible events in spare and unadorned prose. Characters' thoughts and feelings are rarely expressed and thus remain layered and entangled. The narratives' meaning remains latent in the depiction and demands from the reader an act of interpretation. These are, of course, the same qualities that Kermode attributes to all narratives and that, he suggests, account for the indeterminateness of all stories. In biblical narrative, however, Auerbach argues, these latent meanings are combined with a second distinctive quality, a "tyrannical" claim to truth.

> The world of the Scripture stories is not satisfied with claiming to be a historically true reality—it insists that it is the only real world, is destined for autocracy. . . . Far from seeking, like Homer, merely to

make us forget our own reality for a few hours, it seeks to overcome our reality: we are to fit our own life into its world, feel ourselves to be elements in its structure of universal history.[10]

Those two elements, Auerbach asserts, create a tension that reaches its breaking point in the modern era, when the acknowledgment of the Bible's literary qualities increasingly entails a denial of its claim to truth. Obscure narratives with latent meanings cannot, so the modern wisdom goes, claim absolute authority over our attempts at interpretation. Thus emerges the dichotomy that Kermode so clearly sets before us.

The witness of those diverse voices speaking against the possibility of an authoritative reading of a text, particularly a biblical text, is certainly impressive. But I want to suggest that despite the apparent persuasiveness of the arguments Kermode, Auerbach, and others have presented, we do not have to accede either to interpretive relativism or to the political and moral relativism such a position might entail. Nor must we accept the bleak vision that narratives yield only obscure tales and unfollowable worlds. The very literary qualities that Auerbach notes serve not to undermine but to *define* the Bible's authority.

SCRIPTURE'S PROMISE

Scripture, I will argue, presents a complicated but finally coherent narrative that invites the reader to consider the world there depicted as the one true reality. Scripture's claim to truth comes not in the form of a tyrannical dogmatic assertion but in the form of an invitation, or better, a promise. The text's authority lies not in its ability to coerce or compel but in its ability to persuade and convince the reader that the promise it presents is trustworthy. Like all such pledges, the Bible's storied promise can be accepted or denied; the promiser can be accepted as trustworthy or rejected as deceptive. Whether or not the reader chooses to follow, the world depicted in this narrative is surely followable; and that among other things makes the biblical story a most promising tale.[11]

In his path-breaking book *The Eclipse of Biblical Narrative,* Hans Frei noted that post-Reformation interpreters of the Bible failed to see the theological significance of the "realistic or history-like" features of biblical narrative, because they lacked an "appropriate analytical or interpretive procedure" for identifying and employing those features.[12] In *The Identity of Jesus Christ* Frei pioneered the use of intention-action models in order to analyze the realistic aspects of the Gospels' story about Jesus.

This "experiment in Christology" constituted the first step in the development of the required "analytical procedure" for the interpretation of realistic biblical narrative.[13] Several other theologians and philosophers of religion have attempted to refine and extend Frei's work,[14] even though Frei himself seems to have moved in other directions.[15]

The most important work, in addition to Frei's own, on the literary analysis of biblical narrative is Robert Alter's *The Art of Biblical Narrative*. Alter has developed a method of analysis that gives careful attention to the intricate literary patterns of narration, characterization, and techniques of repetition that constitute the biblical texts' literary unity. By attending to both the microscopic and macroscopic aspects of the texts, Alter helps us draw nearer to the goal of stating clear textual warrants for the description of an overarching biblical narrative.

Attention to such features leads not to a more "imaginative" reading of biblical narrative but to a more precise one; and because all these features are linked to discernible details in the Hebrew text, the literary approach is actually a good deal less conjectural than the historical scholarship that asks of a verse whether it contains possible Akkadian loanwords, whether it reflects Sumerian kinship practices, whether it may have been corrupted by scribal error.[16] Precisely in discovering the *literary* art of the biblical narrative, the interpreter begins to approach the elusive goal of discerning rational controls for the interpretation of ancient texts.

One of the most important contributions of Alter's work is to show that the latent and indeterminate quality of biblical narrative does not (*pace* Auerbach) call into question the Bible's authoritative claim, but rather provides the essential clue for understanding the true nature of that claim.

> An essential aim of the innovative technique of fiction worked out by the ancient Hebrew writers was to produce a certain indeterminacy of meaning, especially in regard to motive, moral character, and psychology. . . . Meaning, perhaps for the first time in narrative literature, was conceived as a *process*, requiring continual revision—both in the ordinary sense and in the etymological sense of seeing-again— continual suspension of judgment, weighing of multiple possibilities, brooding over gaps in the information provided. . . . The implicit theology of the Hebrew Bible dictates a complex moral and psychological realism in biblical narrative because God's purposes are always entrammeled in history, dependent on the act of individual men and women for their continuing realization. To scrutinize biblical personages as fictional characters is to see them more sharply in the multifac-

eted, contradictory aspects of their human individuality, which is the biblical God's chosen medium for His experiment with Israel and history.[17]

The world cast up by the Bible's realistic narratives is nuanced and complicated. Like all good stories, biblical narratives are filled with the unexpected, the sudden turn of plot, the coincidence—what Frank Kermode has called "peripeteia."[18] God's intentions and actions are rarely described and almost never depicted. Instead, we are invited to view God's intentions in the actions of human agents, particularly in the actions of the people of Israel and of the man Jesus. Those actions are themselves deeply ambiguous.

Abraham's faithfulness to the God of promise is tested by a heinous demand that he sacrifice his son. Isaac's blessing is passed on to the son who will become the namesake of God's people (Jacob/Israel) through an act of deception. Israel's liberator from slavery is a murderer, and their greatest king is a murderer and adulterer. Yet in and through these ambiguous actions, God is said to be acting. In the New Testament, God is depicted as acting through the agency of Jesus of Nazareth. Yet the Gospel writers show Jesus as uncertain about his own relation to God's reign, as reluctant to exercise his divine authority, as engaging in such unmessianic activities as sharing table fellowship with sinners. The climax of the narrative that purportedly depicts God's ultimate triumph is a story of the betrayal, rejection, and death of Jesus. The meaning of these stories is indeed latent and appears to call forth an act of extraordinary interpretation from the reader.

AN EXTRAORDINARY ACT—FAITH

These stories do indeed call forth an extraordinary act from the reader; Christians call it faith. But faith is neither blind nor irrational. It is an act of intellectual and personal commitment based upon a coherent reading of the biblical narratives. Faith is not the necessary or inevitable response to these texts, nor is the interpretation upon which this commitment is based the only possible way of reading these stories. Faith not only accepts narrative obscurity; it presupposes that the meaning of these narratives is latent within their rich and nuanced depictions. But in responding with faith, the reader recognizes a followable world within these texts and accepts an invitation to enter that world. In so responding, the faithful reader becomes a disciple who acknowledges that the chief character in these stories (and the one who issues the invitation to faith and discipleship) is God. Such acceptance may appear to be a futile act based upon an implausible claim, particularly because God is rarely depicted in these stories and almost never engages the reader in direct address. I want to argue, instead, that this claim is ironic but true. Precisely in upsetting our expectations about how a god ought to be revealed, these stories introduce readers to Yahweh, God of promise who has raised Jesus from the dead.

Two brief examples must suffice to illustrate the way illumination emerges from obscurity in biblical narrative. The Hebrew Bible offers two apparently contradictory accounts of David's accession to kingship.[19] In the first (1 Samuel 16), God is clearly in control of events, summoning Samuel at the outset of the chapter to go to the household of Jesse the Bethlehemite, "for I have provided for myself a king among his sons" (16:1). Samuel proceeds to Bethlehem but is not told which of the sons he is to anoint as king. Indeed, as he encounters Eliab, the oldest and strongest of Jesse's sons, Samuel assumes that he must be the chosen one of God. But God addresses Samuel and explains the difference between appearance and reality: "For Yahweh sees not as man sees; man looks on the outward appearance, but Yahweh looks on the heart" (16:7). Having learned his lesson, Samuel rejects the first seven sons, until finally Jesse sends for the youngest, David, who "is keeping the sheep" (16:11). Yahweh specifically directs Samuel to anoint David, "and the Spirit of Yahweh came mightily upon David from that day forward" (16:13). At the same time, "the Spirit of Yahweh departed from Saul, and an evil spirit from Yahweh tormented him" (16:14). David is then appointed Saul's armor bearer, but his effective role is a reflection of the fact that he bears the Spirit of Yahweh. "And whenever the evil spirit from God was upon Saul, David took the lyre and played it with his hand; so Saul was refreshed, and was well, and the evil spirit departed from him" (16:23).

The second telling of the David story contradicts the first in many details and is notable for the virtual absence of God from the narrative. In this long and detailed account, we have a rich example of "realistic narrative." The story "adopts a style that draws us at once into the thick of historical experience."[20] David is portrayed as an epic hero who through his courageous exploits earns his recognition as king. He slays Goliath and wins the accolades of all Israel. He marries Saul's daughter and develops a deep friendship with Saul's son, precisely as the king turns against David and seeks to kill him. David flees from Saul's wrath, and the two enemies have a series of dramatic encounters during which each spares the life of the other. Finally, Saul is defeated in battle by the Philistines, and both Saul and Jonathan are killed. God's role in bringing these events to fruition is never mentioned throughout the lengthy narrative cycle. At the end of twenty long and exciting chapters, following the murder of Saul's son Ishbosheth, David is finally anointed king by the tribes assembled at Hebron. Though David has apparently earned this honor by his valiant action, the tribes remind David (and the reader) of God's hidden but active presence in these events: "In times past, when Saul was king over us, it was you that led out and brought in Israel; and Yahweh said to you, 'You shall be shepherd of my people Israel, and you shall be prince over Israel' " (2 Samuel 5:2).

The reference to Yahweh seems almost gratuitous unless the reader sees the previous twenty chapters in the context of the first telling of the story in 1 Samuel 16. By juxtaposing these two apparently contradictory stories, the "writer"' is able to give witness to the complicated reality of a world in which historical agents are the vehicles for God's action. Through his role as chief character in this realistic story, David simultaneously enacts his own intentions and those of God.[21] Though in form and content the latter narrative is far more subtle and detailed, it reinforces the simple truth of the first story—that Israel's destiny is controlled by Yahweh's action. Both forms of narration are necessary to depict Yahweh's identity—a God who brings order from chaos both through God's magisterial word and through God's careful forming of human shape from the soil. God is not so much absent from as hidden within the biblical narrative. "God's promise to fulfill a design in history" is enacted in "the brawling chaos of historical experience."[22] The world illumined by the biblical narrative has all the complexity and untidiness of historical reality, but it is for precisely that reason an inhabitable world.

The Gospel of Matthew is characterized by a similar pattern of identification through hiddenness. Except for a few key events (e.g., Jesus' baptism and transfiguration) God is not a primary actor in Matthew's narrative; rather God remains hidden within the actions of Jesus, who takes center stage in the Gospel drama. God's hiddenness is, however, an essential element of the New Testament message; for as readers discover the true identity of Jesus, they recognize that through this narrative God is inviting them to enter into a life of faith and discipleship.

The Gospel writer manipulates various techniques of emplotment and characterization in order to display the relation between Jesus and those who respond to his ministry, crucifixion, and death. As the Gospel's plot develops toward its climax in Jesus' crucifixion and resurrection, the reader is slowly drawn into the story through identification with those who respond to the unfolding of Jesus' identity. Precisely as Jesus' identity becomes fully manifested within the concluding events of the narrative, the flow of the action turns outward toward the reader, who is invited to become a character in this ongoing story. The author provides no final closure to the narrative, its unfinished quality allowing for continuation of the story in the lives of the reader.

In the Gospel's earliest chapters, Jesus is identified solely by reference to his mission. He is "Son of God" (a title accorded to Israel's kings), who has the unique role of saving "his people from their sins" (1:21). Matthew avoids all techniques of verisimilitude in these early chapters in order to identify Jesus simply as the fulfiller of Israel's promises, the one who enacts the saving intentions of the Father. The reader is thus presented with a stylized, almost symbolic, figure, the Son of God, who is clearly linked to Israel and Israel's God. But of the personal individual identity of Jesus, the reader knows virtually nothing.

In the middle chapters of the Gospel, Matthew begins the gradual depiction of Jesus' personal identity. As this section of the narrative unfolds, however, Jesus' relation to God becomes ambiguous. Precisely as Jesus begins to act as an agent in his own right, his relation to God's intentions becomes unclear. How can this "carpenter's son" be "the Christ, the son of the living God"? Matthew signals this ambiguity by displaying a wide range of responses to Jesus' teaching and healing ministry.

In Matthew 9, a paralytic is brought to Jesus: "When Jesus saw their faith he said to the paralytic, 'Take heart, my son; your sins are forgiven' " (9:2). The scribes who overhear these words are shocked at this apparent act of blasphemy (9:3). The other onlookers who observe the miracle of healing have a startled but ambivalent response: "When the crowds saw it, they were afraid, and they glorified God, who had given such authority to men" (9:8).

These three reactions are typical of the responses to Jesus' ambiguous ministry. The scribes and other leaders have a growing sense of outrage at Jesus' presumptive blasphemous behavior. They recognize that Jesus is exercising the authority granted only to the Son of God, but cannot accept that he is the true inheritor of the promises to Israel: "With them is indeed fulfilled the prophecy of Isaiah which says: 'You shall indeed hear but never understand, and you shall indeed see but never perceive' " (13:14). The crowds continually marvel at Jesus and identify him as healer, teacher, the carpenter's son, and one who has authority, but never as Son of God. The identification of Jesus with the saving mission of the Son of God is made by only a few marginal characters in the Gospel narrative: a leper (8:2), a Roman centurion (8:10), the Gadarene demoniacs (8:29), a paralytic (9:2), a hemorrhaging woman (9:22), two blind men (9:29), a Canaanite woman (15:28), the woman in the house of Simon the leper (26:13), and the centurion at the foot of the cross (27:54). These outcasts and sinners alone respond with faith to Jesus' ministry.

The disciples play a particularly ambiguous role throughout the Gospel narrative. In 8:18–22, Matthew skillfully pairs the inquiry of a "scribe" concerning discipleship with that of a "disciple." Both are shown to have a false or incomplete understanding of the demands of Jesus' call. In the story immediately following (23–27), Jesus calls the disciples "men of little faith" when they show fear in the midst of a storm. Their response to Jesus' act of calming the tempest anticipates the reaction of the crowds in the succeeding chapter: "What sort of man is this, that even winds and sea obey him" (8:27)? The disciples, like the scribes and the crowds, neither respond to Jesus' ministry with an act of faith nor recognize him as Son of God.

Even after Jesus grants the Twelve "authority over unclean spirits" (10:1) and shares with them "the secrets of the kingdom of heaven" (13:11), they still do not grasp the full significance of their call to discipleship. In chapter 14, Matthew constructs a second storm story in which Peter seeks to respond to Jesus' call but fails "when he saw the wind" (14:30). Once again, Jesus calls his would-be disciple "man of little faith" (14:31). In the following chapter, Matthew contrasts Peter's behavior to that of a persistent Canaanite woman whom the disciples seek to send away: "O woman, great is your faith!" (15:28).

Significantly, the theme of "little faith" is struck once more in the story of the confusion concerning bread (16:5–12), a vignette Matthew juxtaposes to his account of Peter's confession (13–20). In that latter story, all the conflicting responses to Jesus' identity come together in the person of Peter. Peter becomes the first disciple to confess that Jesus is Son of God (16:16), but then immediately objects to Jesus' foretelling his suffering, death, and resurrection (16:22). For failing to understand that Jesus' sonship and his followers' discipleship entail the cross, Peter, the blessed confessor, is condemned as a Satanic hindrance to Jesus' mission (16:23).

At this point in the narrative, the reader can see the variety of responses that Jesus' ministry elicits. Confusion, wonder, offense, and faith are all possible reactions not only for the characters in the story but for the reader of the text. But in the midst of the ambiguity and uncertainty, one coherent pattern has emerged. To identify Jesus as Son of God—that is, to recognize Jesus as an agent enacting God's saving intentions—is to identify with those who live on the margins of society. And to follow Jesus' invitation to faith and discipleship is to embark on a journey of self-denial, cross bearing, and death. The text may be coherent and the world followable, but the path illumined by this text is hard, narrow, and fraught with danger. The demands of discipleship are far more daunting than the problems associated with hermeneutical obscurity!

The Gospel's concluding section brings these various themes together in a remarkable realistic narrative that summons the reader to enter the world of the text. Jesus' passion is inaugurated in the home of an outcast, Simon the leper. There an unnamed woman anoints Jesus with oil in preparation for burial (26:12). The disciples are "'indignant'" at the waste of oil, but Jesus replies with an extraordinary claim: "Truly, I say to you, wherever this gospel is preached in the whole world, what she has done will be told in memory of her" (26:13). This intriguing story provides the initial frame for the entire passion story, a story that ends with Jesus' body being hurriedly placed in the tomb of Joseph of Arimathea, apparently without proper preparation. Matthew, however, in contrast to Luke, does not have the women who approach the grave on the day after the Sabbath bear spices. Mary Magdalene and the other Mary come simply "to see the sepulchre" (28:1), because the unknown woman had already prepared Jesus for burial. At this early point in the passion story, the unknown woman alone among Jesus' followers recognizes the destiny that awaits this Son of God. She thus provides a contrasting witness to that of Peter, who confesses Jesus' Sonship with his mouth but cannot bear the suffering consequences of that confession.

Indeed, throughout the passion narrative, the women remain the silent followers of the crucified Messiah. They are the only witnesses to the crucifixion (27:55–56). Mary Magdalene and "the other Mary" go along to the sepulchre, hear the announcement of the angel, and then become the first witnesses of the risen Christ (28:9). Matthew describes their unequivocal reaction to Jesus' appearance: "And they came up and took hold of his feet and worshiped him" (28:9). By contrast, the male disciples function more to disrupt than to enhance Jesus' mission. They fall asleep in Gethsemane; one of them betrays him; another denies he even knows him; all of them forsake him and flee at the moment of his arrest. None of them are numbered among those who witness the crucifixion. Consequently, the Son of God is forced to face his final destiny alone. In those final gripping scenes of the passion story, Matthew ironically places the confession of Jesus' identity as Son of God in the mouths of those who seek to destroy him: Caiaphas (26:63), the taunting crowds (27:39, 43), and the Roman centurion (27:54). Though they do not recognize what they have said, they acknowledge that the true Son of God must be a crucified Messiah.

Matthew brings his Gospel to a close with a story that shifts the flow of the narrative into the world of the reader.

> Now the eleven disciples went to Galilee, to the mountain to which Jesus had directed them. And when they saw him they worshiped him; but some doubted. And Jesus came and said to them, "All authority in heaven and on earth has been given to me. Go therefore and make disciples of all nations, baptizing them in the name of the Father and of the Son and of the Holy Spirit, teaching them to observe all that I have commanded you; and lo, I am with you always, to the close of the age.
>
> (28:16–20)

This beautifully crafted scene, which juxtaposes Jesus' promise to the doubting response of his disciples, functions to carry the world of the Gospel narrative into that of the reader. Matthew devises no dramatic confession of faith to conclude his story, nor does he introduce an explicit narrator to proclaim the Gospel's message. Rather, he uses Jesus' final act of promising to extend the Gospel's promise "to the whole world." Jesus, whose identity is depicted in the Gospel's narrative, now becomes the agent of promise as this story becomes a proclamation addressed to the reader. It is as if in this final episode Jesus directs his gaze for the first time outside the frame of the story and issues his promise directly to the reading audience. Thus the reader is invited to respond to this promise by entering the world of the text and joining with those on the mountain who worship him.

Matthew creates "narrative space" for his readers within the Gospel story by reminding them that the fellowship of the disciples has been reduced in number. Only eleven of those originally called to follow still remain, and some of them continue to doubt. In addition, some not originally numbered among the Twelve have taken on the responsibilities of discipleship. The women alone continue to follow him during the events of the passion and are the recipients of the angel's proclamation of his resurrection. Joseph of Arimathea, though not previously identified as one of the Twelve, is called "a disciple of Jesus" when he asks for the body. Thus the opportunity remains for the reader to join the company of disciples by responding in faith and undertaking the journey of discipleship.

By refusing to provide premature closure for his story, Matthew allows the narrative discourse to flow from the text to the reader. The reader who responds in faith is incorporated into the world of the narrative, and the story continues through the community created by this narrated promise. Precisely as the narrative provides definitive identification of Jesus as Son of God, it also extends an invitation to those who read this story. To recognize Jesus as Son of God is to join those who worship Jesus on the mountain and undertake the arduous journey of faith and discipleship.

Do these biblical stories present a coherent narrative that illumines a followable world? I have tried to show that these stories are coherent and that they function to invite the reader into the world of the tale. Whether the world we are invited to enter is inhabitable is not a question that admits of a general answer. That the reader may refuse to accept this story as God's personal promise of salvation is a possibility with which the text itself reckons. Moreover, the event that establishes both God's identity and the narrative's promise is Jesus' resurrection. To acknowledge this narrative as God's promise is to confess that Jesus, the crucified, now lives. That confession requires an act of faith that contradicts ordinary experience concerning the finality of death. The Gospel narrative can be God's promise if, and only if, God has raised Jesus from the dead. The Gospel's claim to truth thus demands acceptance of a deeply paradoxical claim that lies at the heart of the narrative's meaning.

A reader who takes the biblical narrative as God's personal promise has performed an intelligible act based on a coherent reading of the text. *How* the reader comes to such a decision is a complex matter not easily subject to either hermeneutical or theological analysis. The act of coming to believe is a person-specific act with both reasons and causes related to that person's individual history. Theology ought not seek to devise an explanatory theory for the subjective conditions for the possibility of faith, for such theories obscure both the diversity and the mystery of human response to the gospel. To acknowledge the biblical narrative as God's promise is to believe that the crucified Jesus lives. Theology can explain neither why nor how persons come to believe such a paradoxical claim. Theology can only show that the sense of the biblical text does imply that assertion. If a reader does hear the biblical narrative as God's promise, theology can indicate that such a response is warranted, given the content, force, and context of scripture. But the ultimate explanation of that mysterious movement from unbelief to faith lies beyond theology's descriptive competence. Whether the Gospel's followable world leads to its promised end, we cannot know with certainty now, for "we see through a glass darkly." Whether this promising tale leads us through that door into a world of light we can know only if and when "we see face to face." For now we have only faith and discipleship and the identity of one who bids us come and follow. And for some, that is enough.

NOTES

1. Franz Kafka, *The Trial* (New York: Vintage Books, 1956), 267–269.

2. Frank Kermode, *The Genesis of Secrecy: On the Interpretation of Narrative* (Cambridge: Harvard University Press, 1979), 28, 45, 145.

3. Hans W. Frei uses the arguments of the deconstructionists to challenge the hermeneutical tradition in "The 'Literal Readings' of Biblical Narrative in the Christian Tradition: Does It Stretch or Will It Break?" in *The Bible and the Narrative Tradition* (New York: Oxford University Press, 1986), 36–77.

4. Friedrich Nietzsche, "The Gay Science," *The Portable Nietzsche* (New York: Viking Press, 1954), 95.

5. Richard Bernstein, *Beyond Objectivism and Relativism: Science, Hermeneutics, and Praxis* (Philadelphia: University of Pennsylvania Press, 1983), 18.

6. Richard Rorty has shown that the notion of "foundations of knowledge" follows quite naturally from the use of visual epistemological metaphors. If we think of knowledge as a privileged relation to the objects propositions are about, then "we will want to get behind reasons to causes, beyond argument to compulsion from the object known, to a situation in which argument would be not just silly but impossible, for anyone gripped by the object in the required way will be *unable* to doubt or to see an alternative. To reach that point is to reach the foundations of knowledge." Richard Rorty, *Philosophy and the Mirror of Nature* (Princeton: Princeton University Press, 1979), 159.

7. The existential importance of the search for the foundations of knowledge is evident not only in Nietzsche but in the father of the foundational strategy, René Descartes. In describing his reaction to his exercise in methodic doubt, Descartes writes in the Second Meditation, "I feel as though I were suddenly thrown into deep water, being so disconcerted that I can neither plant my feet on the bottom nor swim to the surface." René Descartes, *Discourse on Method and Meditations* (Indianapolis: Library of Liberal Arts, 1960), 81.

8. Among the best discussions of philosophical foundationalism are William P. Alston, "Two Types of Foundationalism," *Journal of Philosophy* 73 (1976): 165–185; Wilfred Sellars, "Empiricism and the Philosophy of Mind," in *Science, Perception, and Reality* (London: Routledge & Kegan Paul, 1963), 127–196; Richard Rorty, "Intuition," in *The Encyclopedia of Philosophy,* vol. 3 (New York: Macmillan, 1967), 204–211; and Rorty, *Philosophy and the Mirror of Nature.* For discussions of foundationalism and religious belief, see Alvin Plantinga, "Is Belief in God Rational?"in *Rationality and Religious Belief,* ed. C. F. Delaney (Notre Dame: University of Notre Dame Press, 1979), 7–27; Jeffrey Stout, *The Flight from Authority* (Notre Dame: University of Notre Dame Press, 1981); and Nicholas Wolterstorff, *Reason Within the Bounds of Religion* (Grand Rapids: Eerdmans, 1976). The two most

thorough discussions of foundationalism and theology are Francis Schüssler Fiorenza, *Foundational Theology* (New York: Crossroad, 1985), esp. 285–310; and Ronald F. Thiemann, *Revelation and Theology: The Gospel as Narrated Promise* (Notre Dame: University of Notre Dame Press, 1985), esp. 1–91.

9. Erich Auerbach, *Mimesis: The Representation of Reality in Western Literature* (Princeton: Princeton University Press, 1953), 12.

10. Ibid., 15.

11. I will use the phrase "biblical story," even though I have not produced the exegetical arguments to justify that rather sweeping term. In this article I will offer only two illustrations of the Bible's narrative art as support for my argument that scripture portrays a followable world. For a more detailed exegetical justification of my argument, see Thiemann, *Revelation and Theology*, 112–156. In order to justify my case more fully, I would need to show that the themes I identify in these biblical narratives are reflected more broadly throughout the canon. Although I believe that a case can be made, I have not yet undertaken that more complex exegetical task. For now, the David cycle and the Gospel of Matthew constitute the core of what I expect to be an expanding "working canon." For my use of that phrase, see David Kelsey, *Uses of Scripture in Recent Theology* (Philadelphia: Fortress Press, 1975), 100–108.

12. Hans W. Frei, *The Eclipse of Biblical Narrative* (New Haven: Yale University Press, 1974).

13. In addition to the works already cited, see Thomas Tracy, *God, Action, and Embodiment* (Grand Rapids: Eerdmans, 1984).

14. See Frei, "The 'Literal Reading' of Biblical Narrative in the Christian Tradition." In this essay, Frei argues that the *sensus literalis* is most appropriately understood as the way the text has been generally used in the community (61–75). This understanding of the "literal sense" moves Frei away from the close textual analysis his earlier work seemed to call for.

15. Robert Alter, *The Art of Biblical Narrative* (New York: Basic Books, 1981), 21. It is important to recognize that Alter does not offer literary analysis as an alternative to historical scholarship. Rather, he sees literary analysis as incorporating the insights of historical-critical investigation. On these points, see Chapter 1.

16. Ibid., 12.

17. Frank Kermode, *The Sense of an Ending* (London: Oxford University Press, 1967), 18.

18. See Alter, *The Art of Biblical Narrative*, 147–154.

19. Ibid., 151.

20. One is reminded of Joseph's comments to his brothers in Genesis 50:20: "As for you, you meant evil against me; but God meant it for good."

21. Alter, *The Art of Biblical Narrative*, 154. In this passage, Alter moves a bit too swiftly from realistic narrative to historical reality. His argument is intended to claim that through the use of the techniques of realistic narrative the biblical writers were able to depict a world fit to the "untidiness" of historical reality.

22. Ibid.

3

THE UNNAMED WOMAN AT BETHANY: A MODEL FOR DISCIPLESHIP

Now when Jesus was at Bethany in the house of Simon the leper, a woman *came up to him* with an alabaster flack of *very expensive* ointment, and she poured it on his head, *as he sat at table. But when the disciples saw it,* they were indignant, *saying,* "Why this waste? For this ointment might have been sold *for a large sum,* and given to the poor. But Jesus, *aware of this,* said *to them,* "Why do you trouble *the woman?* She has done a beautiful thing to me. For you always have the poor with you, but you will not always have me. *In pouring this ointment on* my body *she has done it to prepare me for* burial. Truly, I say to you, wherever this gospel is preached in the whole world, what she has done will be told in memory of her.

(Matthew 26:6–13. Material unique to Matthew is italicized.)

This story of the anointing of Jesus by an unnamed woman in the city of Bethany marks a crucial turning point in the Matthean passion narrative. That narrative begins in chapter 21 with Jesus' entry into Jerusalem: "And when he entered Jerusalem, all the city was stirred, saying, 'Who is this?'" (21:10). With that question, Matthew[1] reiterates the theme of the entire Gospel, which is constructed to answer the question concerning Jesus' identity.

AMBIGUITY IN JESUS' IDENTITY

Throughout the Gospel, Matthew emphasizes the ambiguity inherent in Jesus' identity. In the early chapters (1:1—4:16), Matthew describes Jesus in highly stylized fashion, avoiding all techniques of verisimilitude in order to identify Jesus with the figure Son of God, the one who will "save his people from their sins" (1:21).[2] Throughout the large midsection of the Gospel, Jesus begins to emerge as an agent in his own right, but precisely as he does, his relation to God's intentions becomes unclear. Matthew signals this ambiguity by pointing to the wide range of responses to Jesus' teaching and healing ministry.

The author skillfully manipulates the reactions of the Jewish leaders,[3] the crowds, and the disciples. The crowds marvel at Jesus and identify him as healer, teacher, the carpenter's son, and one who has authority—but never as Son of God. The identification of Jesus with God's saving mission is made by only a few marginal characters in the Gospel narrative: a leper (8:2), a Roman centurion (8:10), the Gadarene demoniacs (8:29), a paralytic (9:2), a hemorrhaging woman (9:22), two blind men (9:29), a Canaanite woman (15:28), and the centurion at the foot of the cross (27:54).

The disciples play a particularly ambiguous role in Matthew's story. Though they respond to Jesus' invitation to follow, they are constantly confused about the nature of Jesus' mission and their own discipleship. On four different occasions, Jesus characterizes them as "men of little faith" (*oligopistoi*). Matthew's literary skill is illustrated by the way in which he places these accounts of the disciples' faithlessness into a broader narrative context. Two of these stories (8:23–27 and 14:22–33) take place "on the sea." In both cases, Jesus and the disciples, pressed in by the crowds, set out for "the other side" (8:18 and 14:22).[4] While in transition on the sea, storms arise, the disciples' faith is tested, Jesus chides them for their doubts, and the storms are stilled.

In the first story, the disciples' response is akin to that of the crowds: "What sort of man is this, that even winds and sea obey him?" (8:27). The disciples, like the scribe and the disciple in the vignettes immediately preceding this story, reveal their false understanding of Jesus' mission and call. By contrast, in the story immediately following, the Gadarene demoniacs "coming out of the tombs" (8:28) recognize Jesus as "Son of God" (8:29). Even those foreigners possessed by demons identify Jesus more easily than those who are his constant companions. In the second story, the disciples' response to Jesus and the storm is more ambiguous. Peter first seeks to join Jesus on the water, but then, "seeing the wind," he begins to sink. He is rebuked as *oligopistis,* but the disciples "in the boat worshiped him, saying, 'Truly you are the Son of God' " (14:33). At the landing, those at Gennesaret recognize Jesus and seek only to "'touch the fringe of his garment; and as many as touched it were made well" (14:36).[5]

The theme of the disciples' confused and insufficient faith continues throughout those stories leading to the passion narrative. Peter's little faith is contrasted to the "great faith" of the Canaanite woman in 15:28. Jesus characterizes the disciples once more as *oligopistoi* (16:8) immediately prior to Peter's confession at Caesarea Philippi. Even that bold recognition of Jesus as "the Christ, the Son of the living God" (16:16) is swiftly undercut by Peter's faithless refusal to recognize that Jesus' Sonship entails that he be "killed, and on the third day be raised" (16:21). For that sudden reversal, the "blessed" (16:17) Peter becomes "Satan" (16:23), the adversary who would tempt Jesus to a false view of Sonship.

AUTHENTIC DISCIPLESHIP

This unflattering depiction of the disciples becomes even more pronounced in Matthew's account of the events surrounding Jesus' passion and crucifixion. The Twelve[6] function primarily to disrupt rather than enhance Jesus' mission. They fall asleep in Gethsemane; one of them betrays him; another denies he even knows him; all of them forsake him and flee at the moment of his arrest. None of them is numbered among those who witness the crucifixion. By contrast, the *women* disciples remain the silent followers of the crucified Messiah. They are the only witnesses to the crucifixion. Mary Magdalene and "the other Mary" go along to the sepulchre, hear the announcement of the angel, and then become the first witnesses of the risen Christ. Matthew describes their unequivocal reaction to Jesus' appearance: "And they came up and took hold of his feet and worshiped him" (28:9).[7]

The female followers of Jesus play a more prominent role in Matthew's Gospel than is usually recognized.[8] Indeed, it can be argued that the women alone function as disciples within the passion narrative, thus effectively replacing the Twelve as the faithful followers of Jesus.[9] As the Gospel narrative develops, there is a subtle but decisive shift in the notion of "discipleship." Precisely as Jesus' role as Son of God is progressively defined through his suffering and death, so also the disciple becomes defined as that faithful follower who identifies with Jesus' ministry and mission. This development is signaled most clearly in a crucial passage in chapter 16.

Immediately following the condemnation of Peter for his refusal to accept Jesus' destiny as the crucified Messiah, Jesus clarifies the true meaning of "following": "Then Jesus told his disciples, 'If any man would come after me, let him deny himself and take up his cross and follow [*akoloutheito*] me. For whoever would save his life will lose it, and

65

whoever loses his life for my sake will find it" (16:24–25). Discipleship and "following" are closely connected throughout the Gospel of Matthew. In each of the call narratives (4:18–22 and 9:9), the mark of discipleship is the willingness of Peter, Andrew, James, John, and Matthew to *follow*. Though Matthew uses the term "disciple" (*mathetes*) to refer to the class of those persons who accompany Jesus during his ministry, the term remains systematically ambiguous. The central section of the Gospel is designed to display the correlative ambiguity between the identity of Jesus and the identity of those who follow. The true followers—the authentic disciples—are those who recognize that Jesus' mission leads to crucifixion, and they embark on a journey that may lead to the loss of their own lives for his sake. Within the passion narrative, only Joseph of Arimathea (27:57) and the women[10] can be identified as authentic disciples.

THE SIGNIFICANCE
OF THE UNNAMED WOMAN'S ACT

In light of this striking role reversal, the story of Jesus' anointing by the unnamed woman at Bethany becomes exceedingly important. This story provides the initial frame within which the events of the passion, crucifixion, and resurrection are narrated. The final frame is provided by the Gospel's concluding narrative, the story of Jesus' command to the eleven to "make disciples of all nations" (28:16–20).

Because Matthew depends upon Mark in his telling of the anointing story, historical critical scholars have tended to overlook important details in Matthew's redactional reshaping of the Markan narrative.[11] Matthew, who in other portions of his Gospel is a skillful realistic narrator, omits some of the detail that gives the Markan story its historylike qualities. He mentions neither the breaking of the flask nor the cost of the ointment (300 denarii, Mark 14:5).[12] The story is thus similar to the tales of the opening section of the Gospel (1:1—4:16), narratives that are notable for the absence of verisimilitude.[13] By forgoing realistic detail, Matthew is able to highlight an important structural element within the story. In the early narratives, Matthew uses this technique to emphasize the significance of the title "Son of God." In the anointing narrative, he is able to focus upon the emblematic act of discipleship this woman performs.

Matthew also gives a more prominent role to the disciples, stressing their indignant response to the woman. Mark does not mention the disciples but simply says, "There were some who said to themselves indignantly, . . . " (14:4). Clearly, Matthew wants to draw attention to the *disciples'* failure to grasp the significance of the woman's act. Once again, the disciples' lack of recognition is contrasted to a woman's insight into the true nature of Jesus' mission: "In pouring this ointment on my body she has done it to prepare me for burial" (26:12). Matthew elaborates upon Mark's much simpler "she has anointed my body beforehand for burying" (14:8) in order to point to the symbolic significance of this act. Not only does the woman recognize that Jesus' mission requires him to face death; she also tacitly acknowledges in concert with the other women of the Gospel that he will "on the third day be raised" (16:21). Matthew alone among the evangelists has the women approach the tomb without bearing spices (28:1), for Jesus has already been prepared for burial by this unnamed woman.

Finally, Matthew reshapes Mark's saying about the poor. In Mark the passage reads: "For you always have the poor with you, and whenever you will, you can do good to them; but you will not always have me" (14:7). Matthew's version sharpens the contrast between Jesus and the poor. "For you always have the poor with you, but you do not always have me" (26:11).[14] What are we to make of this passage? Does it, particularly when combined with the earlier reference to the "poor in spirit" (5:3), indicate a callous disregard for those in poverty? Although such an interpretation is surely possible, I do not think that such disregard is the focus of this text. Indeed, Matthew reconstructs this saying in order to direct the reader's attention to the contrast between "you always have" and "you do not always have." Matthew eliminates Mark's reference to care for the poor for the same reason that he eliminates mention of the broken flask and 300 denarii, that is, in order to focus attention solely upon the interlocked identities of Jesus and this quintessentially faithful disciple. The chiasmic structure of the saying allows Matthew to emphasize the question of Jesus' impending absence, in language that anticipates the final verse of the Gospel ("and lo, I am with you always," 28:20).

MATTHEW'S USE OF "GOSPEL"

"Truly, I say to you, wherever *this* gospel is preached in the whole world, what she has done will be told in memory of her" (26:13). The word *gospel* appears only four times in Matthew. The first two times, it appears in the formulaic phrase "the gospel of the kingdom" (4:23, 9:35). Matthew does not use the word *gospel* again until chapter 24 when, shortly before the passion narrative, Jesus warns of the signs that will accompany "the close of the age" (24:3): "And this gospel of the kingdom will be preached throughout the whole world, as a testimony to all nations; and then the end will come" (24:14).[15] The final use of *gospel* comes in this enigmatic story of Jesus' anointing. In both these final references, Matthew modifies the word *gospel* with the demonstrative *this*.

These broadly separated uses of the word *gospel* capture the progression inherent in Matthew's story. In that section of the narrative in which Jesus' identity remains ambiguous, *gospel* refers to the message that he preaches and enacts in his teaching and healing ministry (4:23; 9:35). It refers as well to the message the disciples proclaim when they are given "authority . . . to heal every disease and every infirmity" (10:1). In none of these cases is the content of the gospel specified; it is simply the "gospel of the kingdom." In the final section of the story, however, as the true identities of Jesus and his authentic disciples emerge, the content of the gospel is more clearly specified. *This gospel* is that good news to be "preached throughout the whole world, as a testimony to all nations" and which when "preached in the whole world . . . will be told in memory of her." This memorial is accomplished when the story of Jesus, *this gospel narrative,* is told in the whole world. When the narrative that identifies Jesus as the crucified Messiah is proclaimed as good news to all nations, this woman, whose act inaugurates Jesus' passion, will be forever remembered, for by her act she identifies herself as a true disciple of the crucified and resurrected Jesus.

EXPANDED DISCIPLESHIP

Matthew brings his narrative to a close with a story that reiterates many of the central themes of the Gospel.

> Now the eleven disciples went to Galilee, to the mountain to which Jesus had directed them. And when they saw him they worshiped him; but some doubted. And Jesus came and said to them, "All authority in heaven and on earth has been given to me. Go therefore and make disciples of all nations (cf. 24:14), baptizing them in the name of the Father and of the Son and of the Holy Spirit, teaching them to observe all that I have commanded you; and lo, I am with you always (cf. 26:11), to the close of the age (cf. 24:3)."
> (28:16–20)[16]

Matthew introduces this final story by reminding his readers that the fellowship of the disciples has been reduced in number. Only eleven of those originally called to follow still remain, and some of them continue to doubt. In addition, some not originally numbered among the Twelve have taken on the responsibilities of discipleship, particularly the women and Joseph of Arimathea. Discipleship is no longer limited to the Twelve; indeed, some of them have forfeited their right to that designation. Rather, those who recognize Jesus as the crucified and resurrected Messiah and take up the responsibilities of following are the true disciples. And those disciples can be found among "all nations." The discerning reader will recognize that the model for such discipleship is to be found in the unnamed woman and those who follow her example.

The unnamed woman thus plays a crucial role in Matthew's narrative strategy of opening the category of "disciple" to those who were not originally among the Twelve. Although the Twelve are not entirely eliminated from discipleship, it is clear by the end of the story, that they no longer *define* the category. Disciples are those who recognize Jesus as the crucified and risen Messiah, who undertake to follow the way of the cross, and who seek to "make disciples of all nations." The opening of discipleship to the "nations" marks a radical shift in the role of the nations within Matthew's Gospel. In chapter 24, the "nations" are those whose warfare will indicate the "sign . . . of the close of the age" (24:3): "Then they will deliver you up to tribulation, and put you to death; and you will be hated by all nations for my name's sake" (24:9). At the end of the Gospel, however, those same "nations" are now candidates for discipleship, and the "close of the age" will be marked by Jesus' continuing presence. This shift in the references to the nations is occasioned by Matthew's depiction of the uncertain role of the Twelve, particularly during the events of the passion. The extension of discipleship to the nations is anticipated by the opening genealogy in which the three women mentioned (Tamar, Rahab, and Ruth) are all "outsiders" who have been grafted onto the tree of Israel. The women function throughout the narrative to point toward the broader scope that "this Gospel" of Jesus will have. And the unnamed woman at Bethany functions symbolically to signal the expansion of the category of discipleship, precisely as she inaugurates Jesus' passion.

This final story of Matthew's Gospel functions to open the world of the text to that of the reader. Matthew creates "narrative space" for his readers within the gospel story through his reference to "the eleven."[17] The reader is reminded that the number of the original disciples has been diminished and that new "followers" have taken their place on the mountain. Matthew devises no final vignette to provide narrative closure for the Gospel; nor does he introduce the explicit voice of the narrator. Rather, he allows Jesus to provide the final words through a statement of direct address. It is as if in this final episode Jesus directs his gaze for the first time outside the frame of the story and addresses his words directly to the reading audience. The language of this final passage resonates with earlier themes to open the possibility of discipleship to those who read this narrative. Thus the reader is urged to respond to this invitation by entering the world of the text and joining with those on the mountain who worship Jesus. In so doing, they will be following the example of that unnamed woman whose act of discipleship is remembered whenever "this gospel is preached in the whole world."

THE LITERARY-THEOLOGICAL APPROACH

The hermeneutical approach exemplified in this rather lengthy ex-egetical exercise is aptly described as "literary-theological." The method seeks to identify intricate patterns of narration, characterization, and linguistic allusion within the text in order to describe the broad theological themes within the gospel story. This approach takes seriously the literary integrity of the final text, but acknowledges as well the multiple sources and strands of tradition identified by historical-critical scholarship. In that regard it bears a close relation to redactional criticism, although it tends to grant a greater degree of literary creativity to the final redactor. In contrast to much historical biblical scholarship (including most redactional criticism), a literary-theological approach has as its primary goal, not the identification of a specific historical context for an individual story or saying, but the redescription of the broad literary and theological themes running throughout the Gospel. Consequently, it attends primarily to the development of plot and character and to various techniques of repetition used within the narrative. By attending to both the microscopic and macroscopic aspects of a text, this approach can help us draw nearer to the goal of stating clear textual warrants for our use of biblical themes within theology.[18] Precisely in discovering the *literary* art of the biblical narrative, the interpreter begins to approach the elusive goal of discerning rational controls for the theological interpretation of ancient texts.

Not only does this approach presuppose certain aspects of historical scholarship; it can also make a contribution to historical criticism by highlighting issues that might not emerge as clearly in an exegetical method that attends primarily to the individual literary unit. I have argued that the theological message of the Gospel of Matthew concerning discipleship cannot be rightly interpreted without careful attention to the role played by women throughout the narrative. The interlocking themes of the faithlessness of the Twelve and the faithfulness of the women are developed with such consistency within the Gospel that the important historical question is raised regarding whether there is a strand of tradition used by the final redactor that highlighted the role of women and questioned or even rejected the place of the Twelve within the company of postresurrection disciples. I do not purport to have an answer to that question, but I am convinced that this literary-theological method allows that issue to be raised with some clarity.

Finally, my hermeneutical approach assumes that various themes within the biblical narratives can be relevant to contemporary Christian life and theology. The appropriation of those themes will always involve an act of critical and imaginative discernment.[19] Texts are inherently ambiguous and patient of multiple readings. The narratives of the Bible are particularly susceptible to variable interpretations because of their peculiar literary qualities.[20] The relevance of a particular biblical theme for contemporary Christian life will depend in part upon the imaginative power of the interpretation and on the context within which that reading is offered. But such contextual factors do not condemn us to a dark hermeneutical night in which all interpretations are gray. Christian communities must still struggle to evaluate rival readings of the biblical texts and seek to determine which readings best illumine our diverse world of experience. In struggling with that ambiguity, we are simply repeating the experience of every generation that has sought to respond to Jesus' call to discipleship. As we continue that struggle, we can be sustained by the confidence that the one we seek to follow has promised to be with us "to the close of the age."

NOTES

1. I will use the name Matthew to refer to the author or final redactor of the Gospel. I am assuming that the redactor worked from various source materials, including the Gospel of Mark, and then reshaped those materials into a distinctive literary and theological document. When I use the word *author,* the word should not be taken as referring to any specific historical person or community. Rather, I mean it in the sense of the "implied author," that is, the "creating person who is implied by the totality of a given work when it is offered to the

world." Wayne Booth, *Critical Understanding* (Chicago: University of Chicago Press, 1979), 269. For a further discussion of the term, see Wayne Booth, *The Rhetoric of Fiction* (Chicago: University of Chicago Press, 1983), esp. 71–76.

2. For a more detailed account of this section of the Gospel, see my *Revelation and Theology: The Gospel as Narrated Promise* (Notre Dame: University of Notre Dame Press, 1985), 115–118.

3. These passages in which Matthew describes the Jewish leaders' rejection of Jesus have been the source for much Christian anti-Judaism and must be interpreted with extreme caution. See Charlotte Klein, *Anti-Judaism in Christian Theology* (Philadelphia: Fortress Press, 1977). Matthew's Gospel was written at a time when Christianity was an emergent Jewish sect contending with other elements in Judaism as rival claimants to the authentic Jewish tradition. The polemic within Matthew cannot be transferred to a situation in which Christianity has become a clearly distinct and numerically dominant religious tradition. For two studies of the problem of the anti-Judaism in Matthew, see Lloyd Gaston, "The Messiah of Israel as Teacher of the Gentiles: The Setting of Matthew's Christology," in *Interpreting the Gospels,* ed. James Luther Mays (Philadelphia: Fortress Press, 1981), and George W. E. Nickelsburg, "Good News/Bad News: The Messiah and God's Fractured Community," *Currents in Theology and Mission* 4, no. 6 (December 1977): 324–332.

4. In chapter 8 the destination is "the country of the Gadarenes"; in chapter 14, Jesus and his disciples cross over "to land at Gennesaret."

5. This phrase clearly alludes to the earlier story of the hemorrhaging woman who touches "the fringe of his garment" and is healed (9:18–22).

6. Matthew's characteristic expression for those disciples who accompanied Jesus on his ministry is "the twelve disciples." He uses "the twelve" as a technical nominative construction only three times (10:5, 26:14, 26:47). The references in chapter 26 are both to Judas, "one of the twelve."

7. Note the contrast with the disciples' reaction to Jesus: "And when they saw him they worshiped him; but some doubted" (28:17).

8. The only thorough analysis of the role of women in Matthew is Janice Capel Anderson, "Matthew: Gender and Reading," *The Bible and Feminist Hermeneutics, Semeia* 28 (1983): 3–27.

9. Norman Perrin, *The Resurrection According to Matthew, Mark, and Luke* (Philadelphia: Fortress Press, 1977), 29–31, makes a similar suggestion with regard to the Gospel of Mark. Jack Dean Kingsbury, "The Verb *Akolouthein* as an Index of Matthew's View of His Community," *Journal of Biblical Literature* 97 (1978): 56–73, argues, however, that the women in Matthew's Gospel are not disciples "in the strict sense." The women and other supplicants are never designated "disciples" (*mathethes*) but rather are described as those who "follow" (*akolouthein*) or "minister to" (*diakonethenai*) Jesus. *Akolouthein,* Kingsbury argues, can be used metaphorically to indicate discipleship only when Jesus speaks, summoning persons to a "personal commitment" that entails the "cost" of self-sacrifice (58). Anderson, "Matthew: Gender and Reading," 18–21, agrees with Kingsbury's assessment: "Although the women play an important part in the narrative, gender seems to prevent their identification as disciples. They are an auxiliary group which can conveniently stand in for the disciples" (20).

10. The women who witness the crucifixion (27:55–56) are identified as the ones "who had followed Jesus" (*ekolouthesan Iesou*).

11. Robert Holst, "The One Anointing of Jesus: Another Application of the Form-Critical Method," *Journal of Biblical Literature* 95, no. 3 (1976): 435–456 makes only two passing references to distinctive Matthean emphases in the anointing narrative in his otherwise thorough analysis of this narrative. Even Elisabeth Schüssler Fiorenza, in her path-breaking discussion in *In Memory of Her* (New York: Crossroad, 1986), fails to note Matthew's peculiar treatment of the story.

12. It is interesting to note that Matthew alone mentions "the thirty pieces of silver" (26:15) in the story of betrayal that follows immediately.

13. For a more complete analysis of these stories, see my *Revelation and Theology*, 115–118.

14. Elisabeth Schüssler Fiorenza has made much of Mark's inclusion of the phrase "whenever you will, you can do good to them": "Thus in remembering that a nameless woman prophet has anointed Jesus as the messianic inaugurator of the *basileia,* the community also remembers that the God of Jesus is on the side of the poor and that God's future, the *basileia,* belongs to the poor" (Schüssler Fiorenza, *In Memory of Her,* 153). This interpretation is less plausible on the basis of the Matthean text, but see n. 16.

15. It is interesting to note that the word *gospel* in both chapters 24 and 26 appears in immediate proximity to the only two uses of the word "betrayal" in Matthew: "And then many will fall away, and betray one another, and hate one another" (24:10); "And from that moment he sought an opportunity to betray him" (26:16). The story of Judas' betrayal follows immediately upon the story of the anointing.

16. This final story is replete with references and allusions that point back to the "this Gospel" passages of chapters 24 and 26. One of the most striking, but least noticed, allusions is to the "have with you/not have with you" contrast of 26:11. In this concluding scene, the one who contrasted his own impending absence to the presence of the poor now pledges, "I am with you always, to the close of the age." I am tempted to argue that the text allows us to connect chapters 26 and 28 through a dialectic play between absence and presence. The "absent" Jesus ("you will not always have me") now promises his "presence" ("lo, I am with you always") precisely in the continuing "presence" of the poor ("the poor you will always have with you"). Matthew is certainly a sufficiently skillful author/redactor to make such a subtle connection, but the textual evidence in support of this interpretation is slim. Although I am attracted to the interpretation, it remains a speculation.

17. Matthew's procedure here bears striking resemblance to the technique of Matthias von Grunewald in his depiction of the crucifixion on the centerpiece of the Isenheimer Altar. In that painting, Grunewald uses the asymmetrical arrangement of the figures at the foot of the cross in combination with the figure of John the Baptist to break the narrative frame of the painting and extend the depiction into the world of the viewer. For a more extended account of this comparison, see my *Revelation and Theology,* 141–143.

18. Robert Alter, *The Art of Biblical Narrative* (New York: Basic Books,

1981), has pioneered the use of this method. His comment about this method's precision is worth quoting: "Attention to such [literary] features leads not to a more 'imaginative' reading of biblical narrative but to a more precise one; and since all these features are linked to discernible details in the . . . text, the literary approach is actually a good deal *less* conjectural than the historical scholarship that asks of a verse whether it contains possible Akkadian loanwords, whether it reflects Sumerian kinship practices, whether it may have been corrupted by scribal error" (21).

19. I have been influenced on this topic by David Kelsey, *The Uses of Scripture in Recent Theology* (Philadelphia: Fortress Press, 1975), and Charles Wood, *The Formation of Christian Understanding* (Philadelphia: Westminster Press, 1981), and *Vision and Discernment* (Atlanta: Scholars Press, 1985). For my criticisms of Kelsey and Wood, see *Revelation and Theology,* 56–70. For my own account of the critical imagination, see "Revelation and Imaginative Construction," *Journal of Religion* 61, no. 3 (July 1981): 242–263, and "Toward a Critical Theological Education," *Harvard Theological Review* 80, no. 1 (January 1987): 1–13.

20. Erich Auerbach, *Mimesis: The Representation of Reality in Western Literature* (Princeton: Princeton University Press, 1953), has, of course, argued that the narratives of Hebrew scripture are "mysterious and 'fraught with background' " (12). Characters' thoughts and feelings are rarely expressed and thus remain layered and entangled. The narratives' meaning remains latent within the depiction and demands from the reader an act of interpretation. Frank Kermode, *The Genesis of Secrecy* (Cambridge: Harvard University Press, 1979), has developed that observation into a theory of narrativity that suggests that all narratives are inherently obscure, "hopelessly plural, endlessly disappointing" (145). Although I find Auerbach's observation accurate, I am not convinced by Kermode's attempt to develop a theory of "narrative obscurity." For further reflections on this theme, see Ronald F. Thiemann, "Radiance and Obscurity in Biblical Narrative," in *Scriptural Authority and Narrative Interpretation* (Philadelphia: Fortress Press, 1987).

4

KARL BARTH AND THE TASK OF CONSTRUCTING A PUBLIC THEOLOGY

The centennial observation of Karl Barth's birth (1886) provided a happy opportunity to reassess the significance of the Swiss theologian's work. Such a reappraisal has been sorely needed, because American theologians since the 1960s have tended to dismiss Barth as a once influential figure in a now discredited theological movement called "neoorthodoxy."[1] Setting aside the oddity of a classification that lumps together such diverse thinkers as Barth, Brunner, Bultmann, Tillich, and the Niebuhrs, this easy dismissal hardly does justice to the man who produced the most wide-ranging theological work of the twentieth century, *The Church Dogmatics*.

In this chapter I will assess Barth's importance for contemporary theology by first viewing his thought in the context of the disputes surrounding the promulgation of the Barmen Declaration. Through an analysis of the criticisms directed against Barth by his conservative German Lutheran opponents of the 1930s, I will seek to show the ecumenical significance of Barth's work for theology in the 1990s. My introductory comments will focus on the Protestant tradition, because the theological and political disputes of those years were carried on in isolation from the Roman Catholic community.[2] The issues raised in that Reformed-Lutheran squabble in those early years of the Third Reich have, however, a continuing significance for contemporary Christian theologians from the full spectrum of confessional traditions.

THE BARMEN DECLARATION

The Barmen Synod of May 1934 and its famous declaration were primarily the result of the efforts of Reformed theologians. Karl Barth's essay "Theologische Existenz Heute!" launched the confessional protest movement against state interference in church affairs.[3] Although Martin Niemoeller, a Lutheran pastor, founded the "Pastor's Emergency League," the impetus for a confessional synod was provided by those free Reformed churches that first met in Barmen in January 1934 and issued a statement of theological confession and protest authored by Karl Barth.[4] The subsequent confessional synod met on May 29–31 at the Reformed Church of Barmen-Gemarke, and Barth, of course, authored the document we now know as the Barmen Declaration. Though Lutheran theologians and pastors were involved in the preparations for the Barmen Synod, their direct contributions were rather limited. In fact, Barth reported that he wrote a first draft of the theological declaration while his two Lutheran cohorts, Thomas Breit and Hans Asmussen, took three-hour-long naps! With some glee, Barth described the occasion. "The Lutheran Church slept and the Reformed Church kept awake. . . . I revised the text of the six statements fortified by strong coffee and one or two Brazilian cigars."[5]

Although Barth's account of Lutheran inaction was somewhat exaggerated, there can be no doubt that Barmen's chief critics were conservative Lutheran theologians. Lutheran opposition to the declaration surfaced even before the synod met. Hermann Sasse, one of the members of the Reich Council of Brethren, which organized the Barmen Synod, refused to endorse the declaration because he believed that Lutheran and Reformed churches possessed insufficient doctrinal unity to issue a joint confession. Paul Althaus and Werner Elert, professors of systematic theology on the influential Lutheran faculty at Erlangen, were among the leading theological critics of the declaration and were responsible for the creation of the Lutheran Council, a mediating "third front" in the German Church Struggle, which drained valuable Lutheran support away from the Confessing Church.[6]

The Lutheran objections to Barth and Barmen were primarily theological and focused on the declaration's apparent rejection of the revelatory content of God's law. The well-known first article of the declaration affirms Jesus Christ, "the one Word of God," to be the sole source of God's revelation.[7] To German Lutheran ears, that sounded like a familiar sixteenth-century Reformed heresy. Werner Elert's assessment of that teaching is characteristically blunt:

> That the Barmen Confession is a point-blank, provocative repetition of the antinomian false teaching of the Reformation will be immediately clear to anyone who stands not on the ground of Barmen but

> on that of the Lutheran confessions. . . . This explicit antinomian heresy . . . is not a peripheral lapse of the Barmen Confession. It reveals far more the sense and intention of the entire Confession. This teaching is fundamental also for the entire ecclesiastical and church-political position of the Barmen Synod.[8]

Those are serious charges, "fightin' words" one might say, and they raise issues that are worthy of serious theological discussion and debate. But Elert issued this challenge in June of 1934, a full seventeen months after Hitler assumed the chancellorship, nine months after the German Christian, Ludwig Muller, was elected Reich bishop, just eight months after Reinhold Krause's scurrilous anti-Semitic Sports Palace address, and a scant three months after the promulgation of the first of the Nuremberg laws. One might well ask whether this was the time to be raising questions about fine points of theological doctrine. And that is precisely what Elert's fellow Lutheran, Hans Asmussen, asked in a scathing response written just weeks after Elert's original attack on the declaration.

> Excuse me, Herr Professor, for bringing to your attention the latest news. For the last year thousands of pastors have had their existence as Christian preachers threatened, thousands of congregations have had their existence as Christian communities threatened. We find ourselves in a raging sea after a shipwreck. A sea-worthy ship is nearby, ready to rescue the shipwrecked. Believe me, those who have been shipwrecked will not jump into the water again, because an engineer on the land has shown that in his opinion our ship's mast is slightly askew.[9]

Asmussen then turns his ire directly on the dry and secure theological engineer for his failure ever to criticize the Deutsche Christen:

> Violence, injustice, and false teaching were never sufficient grounds earlier for him to declare war on the other side. He won't even address us theologically. Otherwise he would have at least taken the trouble to read the Barmen Declaration properly. He wants war! Then let him have it! If God has allowed the confessing front to be formed without him, so also God will preserve it against him.[10]

By the end of 1938, however, the confessing front had been effectively eliminated as a force for nonconformism in the Third Reich. Hemmed in by legislative strictures devised by the Nazis and torn by internal strife, the Confessing Church so disintegrated that its leadership offered no word of protest following the horrible events of Kristallnacht in November of 1938.

The reasons for the ultimate collapse of the Confessing Church are many and have not yet been fully analyzed by scholars of the Church Struggle. Eberhard Bethge has argued that by 1938 resistance to the Nazis was possible only in the form of active disobedience against the government, and few in the Confessing Church were willing to engage in such activity. When war was finally declared, Martin Niemoeller was among the first to volunteer for active service, and many Confessing Church pastors followed his lead. Bethge writes that of the hundreds of young confessing pastors with whom he has spoken, there was not one "who had not accepted the draft card as the long-sought opportunity to prove his inner national conviction and to sacrifice himself for the nation as a soldier."[11] German patriotism and nationalism ran deep, even among those who most courageously resisted the theological and church-political threat of the Deutsche Christen.

It may be that no amount of solidarity within the Confessing Church could have withstood the enormous pressures presented by the outbreak of the war. But the fact remains that very few Lutheran theologians and clergy were forced to make the momentous choice that Niemoeller and others had to face. The vast majority of Lutherans had by 1936 accepted the authority of the state-run Ministry for Church Affairs and participated freely in the new national German Evangelical Church. There can be no doubt that the early Lutheran opposition to Barmen seriously weakened the ability of the Confessing Church to serve as a force for nonconformism in German society from 1934–38.

Why were Lutherans like Althaus, Elert, Gogarten, Sasse, and others so unwilling to participate in the confessional movement? Again the reasons are complex and not yet fully obvious even to the most insightful of Church Struggle scholars. Some, like Arthur Cochrane, have ventured opinions. In his influential book *The Church's Confession Under Hitler,* Cochrane writes that "many Lutherans were jealous of the prominent part being played by Reformed Churchmen, and Karl Barth was especially obnoxious to them. . . . Depressing to record is the fact that at a time when the 'house was on fire,' when the very existence of the evangelical Church was at stake, many Lutherans were intent upon preserving institutional Lutheranism."[12] Such charges, though often repeated, hardly do justice to the theological seriousness of Barmen's Lutheran opponents. Their theological objections to Barmen's Barthian Christocentrism were authentic and cannot be dismissed as mere camouflage for positions that were essentially political or church-political in nature. On the other hand, the widespread support for Hitler among German Lutherans and their virulent opposition to the Confessing Church is deeply distressing. The full story of the Lutheran position in the early years of the Church Struggle has yet to be told.

THE ETERNAL COVENANT

It is not my intention to tell that story in this chapter, though I hope my comments might illuminate a part of it. My primary task is a different one, namely, to assess the contemporary significance of the theology of Karl Barth for the task of constructing a public theology. I have begun with this extended introduction, however, because theologians in America have hardly been more supportive of Barth's theology than their German predecessors. Although there have been pockets of support for Barth's theology within American Christianity, most theologians have shared the widespread American view that Barth's opposition to natural theology, his rejection of any systematic connection between theology and philosophy, and his single-minded attention to the doctrine of revelation rendered his theology passé for the American cultural situation. Langdon Gilkey speaks for the majority of mainstream Protestant theologians in the following analysis of Barth's thought.

> [Barth's] theology presupposed a stark and real separation between the Church and the world, between belief and unbelief, between the Word of God and the secular. . . . But the actual situation was by no means characterized by any such clear and distinct separation: the world was within the Church, belief was saturated by secular doubt, and no one, either in pew or pulpit, was sure a divine Word had been heard at all or a divine presence manifested. In such a situation, the theology that was unable to relate itself to ordinary experience was bound to falter—and it did. . . . The present unreality and so seeming impossibility of theological language about God stems fundamentally . . . from this [Barthian] split between our existence in the secular world . . . on the one hand, and a theological language, on the other, that has had no essential touch with that world.[13]

These objections to Barth's theology appear to be vastly different from those conservative, and somewhat parochial, criticisms of Barmen's German Lutheran detractors. And yet, I want to suggest, they share one crucial characteristic. Both sets of criticisms reflect the predominant intellectual and political sentiments of their respective cultures. Althaus and Elert represent that broad cultural tradition of post-Reformation Germany: confessionally Lutheran, politically conservative and monarchial, socially aristocratic. These are the people who found themselves displaced and alienated from the political democracy and cultural freedom of Weimar culture. Writing in 1927, Althaus bemoaned the decadence of the German nation.

> Germany appears everywhere to be painfully degenerate. Our Volk has lost itself . . . [l]ost itself to civilization, lost to foreign ways . . . splintering into the mass instead of membership in the Volk body, a "society" of unbound individuals instead of organic community, uprootedness and homelessness . . . disinheritedness instead of life in the traditions of our fathers . . . the takeover by foreign influences of our literature, theater, art, fashions, and celebrations, of party ways and of public life, our abandonment to Volkless money powers.[14]

As the antidote to these poisonous modern ways, the confessional Lutherans urged a reaffirmation of the God-given unity between the spirit of Lutheranism and that of the German Volk. "The peculiar form that Christianity has taken on in its evangelical aspect," wrote Emanuel Hirsch, "derives from the meeting of German humanity with the Gospel."[15] "The present historical hour" was so crucial because it represented the flowering of that implicit eternal covenant between Lutheranism and the Germanic heritage (*Deutschtum*). Lutheranism was, Althaus argued, the peculiar "German form of religion. . . . The way that Germans conceive of the reality of God and the form of Jesus Christ . . . corresponds in its depths to the Germanic type and makes the German and the Biblical . . . so kindred to each other."[16] Though Althaus later withdrew his support from such Volkish sentiments, he remained wedded to these cultural and political notions at least through 1935.

Contemporary American critics of Barth are also wedded to particular cultural and political conventions of our society. In no way do I want to suggest that the liberal intellectual and political traditions of our culture pose the same kind of dangers as the Volkish ideology of nineteenth- and twentieth-century Germany. In many ways, Barth's liberal American critics stand on the opposite end of the political, religious, and theological spectrum from their German Lutheran counterparts. They would undoubtedly have felt at home in that Weimar culture so alien to the Volkish theologians. Nothing could be more repugnant to these contemporary theologians than the assertion of an eternal covenant between the Christian gospel and a particular national or cultural group. They have embraced the spirit of free inquiry born of the Enlightenment that the Volkish thinkers so feared. Indeed, they most often criticize Barth for his arbitrary and inconsistent use of the tools of critical inquiry. Barth's argument concerning the historicity of the resurrection is, Van Harvey asserts, "either arbitrary or a sacrifice of the intellect. . . . He makes historical assertions on the basis of faith which he then claims no historian has the right to assess. He claims that the bodily resurrection is a guarantee that it was Jesus who appeared to the disciples and yet insists that no historian can, in the nature of the case, assess this claim. . . . Barth, in effect, claims all the advantages of history but will assume none of its risks."[17]

Yet for all their distance from the conservative Germans of the 1930s, Barth's contemporary detractors assert their own form of an "eternal covenant." Langdon Gilkey, Van Harvey, Gordon Kaufman, Schubert Ogden, and David Tracy all submit to some version of that creed first and most powerfully articulated by Friedrich Schleiermacher. "Shall the tangle of history," Schleiermacher asked, "so unravel that Christianity becomes identified with barbarism and science with unbelief? . . . Unless the Reformation from which our church first emerged endeavors to establish an eternal covenant between the living Christian faith and completely free, independent scientific inquiry, so that faith does not hinder science and science does not exclude faith, it fails to meet adequately the needs of our time."[18]

One of the most distinctive aspects of Barth's theology is his adamant refusal to subscribe to either form of the eternal covenant. That refusal has earned him the ire of both his German and American critics. To claims that the Volkish revolution represented the consummation of the divine covenant between Lutheranism and Germanic culture, Barth replied simply, "I continue to do theology, and only theology, as if nothing had happened."[19] To claims that the Christian faith must be eternally yoked with free scientific inquiry, Barth responded with characteristic irony: "Christianity need not accompany barbarism nor scholarship unbelief. Natural science and biblical criticism can come. . . . The little ship of the church in which we are all voyaging is protected against overturning. No war will be declared and no one will be shut out. Is not all this very remarkable? There are only two mourners, the Bible and the Reformation."[20]

I want to argue that <u>Barth's rejection of the notion of any eternal covenant between the Christian faith and science, culture, politics, or philosophy ought not be the basis for a critique of his theology but is in fact the key to an appreciation of Barth's contemporary significance</u>. In repudiating the *eternal* covenant, Barth does not thereby cut all ties between Christian theology and the intellectual and cultural resources of contemporary society. Gilkey and others are simply wrong when they claim that Barth "presupposes a stark separation" between church and world, faith and secularity, theology and culture. Rather, Barth takes the relationships among those pairs to be endlessly fascinating and complex. No single systematic scheme could possibly encompass the variety of relations between theology and culture. No general philosophical ontology could account for the complicated relation between Christian faith and secular self-understanding. Any theology that yokes itself to a systematic philosophy, no matter how general or formal, will inevitably, Barth believed, lose touch with the surprising variety and particularity of God's creation reconciled in Jesus Christ, with the boundless possibilities for interaction between the Christian gospel and contemporary culture. Barth did not eschew philosophy; he simply used it eclectically in service of the Christian faith.

That observation points to a second major reason for Barth's repudiation of the eternal covenant. Barth's reading of the history of modern theology convinced him that any systematic correlation between Christian discourse and the language of culture threatened the independence and integrity of the Christian faith. Christian language does, in its own halting and piecemeal fashion, describe the reality of the world in which we all live, a world whose origin and destiny are determined by the reconciliation accomplished in Jesus Christ. Insofar as the language does truly describe, its irreducible integrity and distinctive logic must be preserved. Because that language describes our common world of experience, it must be related to other forms of human discourse, but the terms of that relation must always be ruled by the logic of the Christian gospel. Though he rejects any eternal covenant between the gospel and culture, Barth willingly adopts a series of *ad hoc* alliances, for example, between theology and philosophy.

But every use of philosophy in theology is for Barth simply the temporary borrowing of a tool to help us better understand the complex meaning of the Christian gospel. Barth's view of the role of philosophy in the development of theological method is strikingly similar to that of a rather surprising colleague, Bill James, a sabermatrician, who writes in the 1984 version of his *Baseball Abstract,* "Methods are roads that one travels on in searching for the truth, and like all roads they can be constructed and abandoned as needed."[21]

I want to argue that Barth's rejection of the eternal covenant is as relevant for our own time as it was for Germany of the 1930s. In the next section of this chapter, I will try to show that Barth's theological argument against the German Christians and their implicit supporters, those whom Barth termed "mediating theologians," is nothing more than an outgrowth of his doctrine of revelation. For Barth, proper speech about

God and appropriate political action go hand in hand. Because Barth developed the theological implications of his view of revelation in much greater detail than the political implications, I will focus on Barth's distinctive contribution to theological method. Then in the following section I will attempt to show why and how Barth's conception of theology remains peculiarly appropriate for a secular and pluralistic culture like our own, in which we struggle to maintain and develop an appropriate sense of Christian identity.

BARTH'S REJECTION
OF THE ETERNAL COVENANT

Late in 1933, Barth offered the following assessment of the theology of the German Christian movement: "Because the teaching and conduct of the 'German Christians' is nothing else than an especially striking consequence of the whole development of modern Protestantism since 1700, the protest is directed against an existing and spreading corruption of the whole evangelical Church."[22] Barth was convinced that the Volkish heresy of the German Christians was not simply an anomalous outbreak of bizarre false teaching, but was rather a consistent development of the neo-Protestant theology begun by Schleiermacher. Moreover, Barth argued that those, like the confessional Lutherans, who refused to join the Confessing Church movement were for all their apparent conservatism infected by the mediating tendencies of neo-Protestantism.

For a long time I believed that charge to be at best an example of Barth's rhetorical bluster and at worst a libelous condemnation of a noble theological tradition. I still believe that Barth's way of arguing his case is wrongheaded and confusing. No historical line can be drawn from Schleiermacher and Ritschl to Joachim Hossenfelder and Emanuel Hirsch. And yet there is, I am now convinced, more to Barth's charge than one might immediately assume. The connections between neo-Protestantism and the Volkish theology of the 1930s are neither as obvious nor as systematic as Barth believed them to be. Indeed, I would argue that the similarities between the movements are limited to a single instance, namely, that both affirm some version of what I have called an eternal covenant between the Christian faith and modern culture. And that similarity is what binds both movements to Barth's contemporary American critics.

Barth's rejection of the eternal covenant is grounded in his distinctive conception of revelation. Although Barth's name and reputation will be forever linked with that doctrine, many accounts of his position tend to blur Barth's distinctive contribution to our thinking about revelation. Unlike those twentieth-century thinkers with whom he is often lumped, the so-called neoorthodox theologians, Barth does not conceive of revelation primarily as the process by which we come to know God. For Barth, revelation denotes the content of our knowledge of God, and his reflections concerning the process by which we come to know have a distinctly secondary status. For Barth, the category of revelation cannot be separated from God's identity, because revelation is nothing other than the being of God in verbal form. It is, to use Barth's own language, the "reiterated being" of God, that is, God's inner-trinitarian being made available in word and history. Thus Barth begins his reflection on revelation in the *Church Dogmatics* with a section entitled "The Place of the Doctrine of the Trinity in Dogmatics."[23] He does that not simply to appear stolid and old-fashioned in a notoriously faddish discipline but because God's revelation *is* God's triune being, or better, God's triune identity. If God is identified solely through revelation, then theology must begin by reflecting upon God's identity, and in Christianity that means beginning with the doctrine of the Trinity.

The human problem to which revelation offers a solution is the problem of proper speech about God. How are we sinful human beings to speak of the holy and transcendent God? Barth captured the essence of that dilemma in his famous 1927 essay "The Word of God and the Task of Ministry." "We ought to speak of God," Barth writes. "We are human, however, and so cannot speak of God. We ought therefore to recognize both our obligation and our inability and by that very recognition give God the glory. This is our perplexity. The rest of our task fades into insignificance by comparison"[24]

In Barth's hands, the quintessential modern question, "How is knowledge of God possible?" takes on a distinctive, almost idiosyncratic shape. Most modern theologians, when faced with that question, have sought to show that human beings possess an innate capacity for relation to God. Knowledge of God is possible, these theologians have argued, because we are creatures made in God's image and thus are fit for relation with God by virtue of our rationality, our ability for self-consciousness and self-transcendence, or our capacity for language, that is, by virtue of some natural human capability. These arguments for *homo religiosus* have a common philosophical structure. Most theologians seek to show by a necessary or transcendental argument that human existence possesses an ontological depth or root that is irreducibly religious.

David Tracy, for example, argues that the religious dimension becomes manifest in certain "boundary" or "limit" situations where, in an ecstatic moment, "we experience a reality simply given, gifted, happened. . . . The objective referent of all such . . . experience is that reality which religious human beings mean when they say 'God.' "[25] To be human is to be religious, and to be religious is to be in relation to God. The possibility for knowledge of God is thus grounded in some universal quality of human being.

Such arguments are clearly manifestations of belief in the eternal covenant. Knowledge of God, or a relation to God, is an eternal human possibility. God and humanity are bound to one another in an eternal covenant grounded in human nature. Barth's rejection of such arguments—that is, his rejection of every form of natural theology—is based on his conviction that the eternal covenant, in all its forms, finally limits the utter graciousness of God. The possibility for knowledge of God, Barth argues, is grounded not in any human capacity or capability but within God's own trinitarian being. The possibility for relation to and knowledge of God is primarily and properly God's own possibility. That assertion once again brings the doctrine of the Trinity to the fore in Barth's thinking. The triune God lives in self-differentiated relation. The differentiated "persons" of the triune reality are unified precisely as they participate in one another. And that participation establishes a relation of mutual love and self-knowledge within God's being *ad intra.* Thus God is knowable *in se,* that is, in God's own inner being. So also God is in loving relation *in se,* independent of any relation to reality external to God. God's knowability is not established by a relation to human beings, for God is knowable *in se.* But God does in an act of sheer grace deign to share that knowability with us. In Christ and in the gospel that proclaims him, God shares with us the possibility that is properly God's own—the possibility for knowledge of God and for a loving relation with God.

How does this trinitarian view of revelation help us address the problem of the possibility of theological language? How does this bold assertion of the priority of God's grace assist us in speaking of God? Barth argues that God's revelation provides the only possible basis for proper speech about God. Because God has become available to us in the one Word, Jesus Christ, we are now enabled to undertake an interpretation of that revelation. Our speech is truly speech about God if we follow the path that God has laid out for us in revelation. Theological interpretation is always an act of faithful obedience in which we submit our powers of mind and imagination to the guidance of the Spirit through the scriptural text that witnesses to Christ.

The interpretive relationship between text and reader is complex, for it involves both the guidance of the Spirit and the free but obedient act of theological interpretation. Thus Barth sometimes speaks of revelation as "God's self-interpretation," almost as if to suggest that our interpretive faculties play no role in understanding that revelation. In the same way, he so stresses our obedient response to revelation that he seems to deny completely any moment of freedom in the interpretive act. So he writes in a wonderful early essay entitled "Fate and Idea in Theology": "Faith is not the kind of knowledge in which we can see ourselves as creative. In this knowledge we must rather see ourselves as obedient. . . . Obedience here must be pure obedience. . . . There can be no question of reciprocity between God's action and our own."[26]

On the other hand, Barth can acknowledge the need for full engagement of our intellectual faculties in the task of interpreting God's revelation. In *Evangelical Theology* he writes: "The central affirmations of the Bible are not self-evident; the Word of God itself, as witnessed to in the Bible, is not immediately obvious in any of its chapters or verses. On the contrary, the truth of the Word must be *sought* precisely, in order to be understood in its deep simplicity. Every possible means must be used . . . not the least, the enlistment of every device of the conjectural imagination."[27]

Theology is for Barth a hermeneutical activity in which the theologian in the context of the Christian community seeks to give, in Hans Frei's helpful phrase, a faithful redescription of the biblical narrative. Theology is a human activity through which God's revelation manifests itself in human speech. "Thinking and speaking humanly, yet nevertheless letting God's Word be said—that is the task of theology. It is the task of a theology which, granted God's grace, thinks and speaks not about [the] boundaries of human thought, but with all possible objectivity about God."[28] Christian theology must always have that dual emphasis on God's guiding grace and free human inquiry, but if priority is to be given (as Barth believes it must) to God's free grace, then the two elements of interpretation can never be systematically correlated. Theology must reflect the dialectical character of the revelation it seeks to redescribe. Our knowing of God must conform to God's knowability, that is, to the very structure of God's being as made known to us in revelation.

Though God can truly be known in our act of interpretation, God remains in sovereign control of God's own knowability. In the act of revelation, God is simultaneously revealed and hidden—revealed because God is truly made available to us, hidden because God remains in sovereign control of that self-manifestation. Because God's prior movement to us is the necessary condition for our knowing, we can discern God's being only in the place where God has freely chosen to share the divine reality with us. Moreover, we can interpret rightly only as we seek to conform our knowing to God's knowability, that is, as we fashion our thinking according to the pattern through which God has become revealed.

Revelation is thus both God's self-interpretation and our interpretation of God. But our interpretation of revelation can be true only as it seeks to conform itself to the pattern and structure of God's being as shown in revelation. Theology is the search to discern the being of God in the words of the biblical text.

Barth, of course, does not simply equate the being of God and the biblical text, for that would be a denial of God's hiddenness. For Barth, all knowledge of God has a "sacramental" quality, because we come to know God through a creaturely medium that is not God, an external reality that God has chosen as the vehicle for revelation, namely, the humanity of the man Jesus. We cannot know God in any and every piece of creaturely reality, but only where God has freely chosen to be revealed. In choosing the humanity of Jesus, God has provided a sacramental and thus indirect access to the divine reality. But there is a further element of indirectness that affects the nature of the theological task.

Jesus Christ as God incarnate is God's sacramental presence among humankind; but even that sacramental presence cannot be known directly, for God is known in Jesus Christ only through the witness of the biblical narrative. As the history of God's action (and thus God's being) in Jesus Christ is narrated in scripture, we come to know the identity of Jesus Christ and thereby to know God. Such knowing and consequent speech of God is a reliable reflection of God, because God's being is always in those Christological acts. But this knowing process is always indirect, and thus theology must always rely on the all too human traits of imagination, intellect, and wisdom as we strive to offer a faithful account of God's revelation in Jesus Christ.

THE WORK OF THE THEOLOGIAN

Theologians will and should continue to have their quarrels with Karl Barth. Those in the Roman Catholic tradition in particular will remain dissatisfied with Barth's refusal to extend his notion of the sacramental to include the earthly elements of bread, wine, water, and words. Barth's adamant restriction of God's sacramental action to the humanity of Jesus will appear to some to be an unhappy restriction of the notion of the church as the body of Christ. So too many theologians will remain cool to Barth's characteristic Reformed emphasis on election and the peculiar Christological ontology that emerges from his distinctive view of God's predestinating activity. As Robert Jenson has so clearly shown, a little more emphasis on promise and futurity offers a salutary corrective to Barth's fascination with primal beginnings.[29] Finally, Barth's "being in act ontology" begs the question of the reality of the God identified in the biblical narrative and consequently introduces a fundamental philosophical confusion into his thought.[30]

But none of these matters, important as they may be, imply a criticism of Barth's basic view of the theological task. On that question, it seems to me, Barth is exactly right. Barth is the great modern defender of the Augustinian/Anselmian view of theology as *fides quaerens intellectum.* Theology in this mode is faith's endeavor through the use of reason to offer a "conceptual redescription of the biblical narrative." Theology in Barth's understanding is located squarely within the Christian community and begins its reflection with the "objective credo" of the Christian church, its confession that God is known in Jesus Christ. For Barth, theology is a hermeneutical task that begins with a text that must be interpreted in the context of a living tradition. But this does not in any sense imply a "stark separation" between church and world or the gospel and human culture. Nor does it mean that contemporary philosophical and cultural resources cannot be used in the theological task. They can and must be used, though they must always be used in a way that allows the distinctive logic of the Christian gospel to guide and shape that use.

It is important to remember that for Barth the hiddenness of God is an inescapable presupposition of theology's hermeneutical task. The theologian's job is to reflect upon that which has been confessed in the church's credo in an attempt to bring the being of God to speech, to trace its internal logic, to redescribe it conceptually. The accomplishment of that task requires an act of human interpretation, and all interpretation requires the use of reason, imagination, and their conceptual and aesthetic resources. Precisely because the knowledge of God is indirect, a space is opened that can only be filled by the imaginative act of the theologian. The theologian does not simply repeat the biblical narrative, but rather interprets it or conceptually redescribes it. For that task, as

Barth himself says, "every possible means must be used," including the resources of philosophy and contemporary culture.

It is this view of theology that, I believe, makes Karl Barth such an important figure for the contemporary theological task. His view of the theologian as one who responds faithfully to God's reconciling grace, his conception of theology as faith seeking understanding, his rejection of any form of the eternal covenant: these are the qualities that establish the continuing significance of Barth's theology. The reasons for Barth's continued relevance are both perennial and contemporary.

His view of theology gives the most appropriate methodological shape to the Christian doctrine of justification. No other contemporary view of theology gives such consistent witness to the primacy of God's grace in the theological task. In his greater Galatians commentary, Luther characterizes the doctrine of justification as follows: "We continually teach that the knowledge of Christ and of faith is not a human work but utterly a divine gift. . . . What the Gospel teaches and shows me is a divine work given to me by sheer grace."[31] I know of no other modern theologian whose work gives such eloquent witness to that perennial Christian teaching as does the theology of Karl Barth.

CONCLUSION

But Barth's theology also offers resources for responding to the peculiar problems of our contemporary age. I want to conclude with a few remarks on that topic. The greatest challenge of post-Enlightenment theology has been to restate the Christian gospel under the changed conditions of the modern world; that is, in an intellectual and cultural atmosphere in which the reality of God, and perforce of God's grace, has been decisively questioned. Not only has the theistic consensus of Christendom collapsed in our day, but powerful nontheistic alternatives have been proposed. Modern theologians are confronted not only by the logical possibility of atheism, but by its apparent instantiation in those who claim with Pascal's interlocutor, "I am so made that I cannot believe."[32]

Most modern theologians believe that the challenge of atheism is most aptly met by once again asserting the eternal covenant between the Christian faith and rationality. The problems with this approach are manifold. I have already discussed some of those difficulties in my treatment of Barth's criticisms of neo-Protestantism, of most importance, the failure of this approach to give sufficient emphasis to the primacy of God's grace. But I want to conclude by suggesting that a theology that asserts the eternal covenant is particularly ill-suited to meet the peculiar problems of our postmodern age.

There is widespread agreement that contemporary Western culture has become radically pluralistic. Most theologians accept cultural, religious, and theological pluralism as the inevitable context within which theology must operate. Yet for all that recognition, celebration, and/or bemoaning of pluralism, there is precious little serious analysis of the nature and consequences of the phenomenon. Clearly, I have neither the space nor perhaps the competence to develop such an analysis here, but I do want to point to an important characteristic of our pluralistic situation that raises serious questions to those theologies committed to the eternal covenant.

Alasdair MacIntyre, in his important books *After Virtue*[33] and *Whose Justice? Which Rationality?*[34] has raised a profound challenge to all philosophers and theologians who seek to affirm a common human essence. Contemporary culture, MacIntyre argues, has become so fragmented that we cannot reach moral agreement on the most basic public issues. People who engage in ethical disputes about abortion or nuclear disarmament or homosexuality cannot reach agreement because they argue from "rival and incommensurable moral premises." Moral disagreement, he asserts, is not simply an accidental result of a faulty process of adjudication; it is inherent in the very nature of contemporary moral disputes. Such disputes *necessarily* resist all efforts at adjudication, precisely because our culture has no common understanding of human nature and destiny. Moral reasoning is in disarray because we lack the one thing needful for genuine moral discussion—a common understanding of the *telos* of human existence.

MacIntyre's position is persuasively argued, and any theologian who would seek to analyze the phenomenon of pluralism must reckon with his radical analysis. Many have criticized the apparent relativistic implications of his argument, and MacIntyre has sought in his most recent work to defend himself against those criticisms. But even MacIntyre's critics acknowledge that his argument, when combined with other philosophical refutations of epistemological foundationalism, render assertions concerning a common human essence deeply suspect.

The depth and persuasiveness of our current moral pluralism makes the assertion of an eternal covenant between theology and culture implausible. The two partners in that relationship are both in a state of disarray, and it is difficult if not impossible to speak of either in a unitary fashion. The goal of establishing some common ground between the

Christian faith and secular rational inquiry is surely a noble one, but at this moment in our history the best we can hope for is a series of temporary and *ad hoc* alliances between theology and the resources of our culture. Any more permanent covenant between, for example, Christian belief and rational inquiry becomes suspect in large part because rational inquiry has increasingly sought to identify itself with unbelief. The defense of atheism by figures like Feuerbach, Marx, Nietzsche, and their twentieth-century descendants has given the new pluralism a powerful intellectual justification. The most basic belief of Christendom, belief in God's existence, has been systematically denied by this tradition of radical atheism. Consequently, we can no longer assume that belief in God is part of our common human heritage.

Nonetheless, contemporary theologians continue to seek to demonstrate the essential religiousness of every human being, thereby reasserting the eternal covenant. Arguments for *homo religiosus* are alive and well, particularly among those theologians most sharply critical of Karl Barth. I have already referred to David Tracy's attempt to offer a transcendental argument that will demonstrate that "God" is "the objective referent" of our limited experiences and language. Even more striking is Schubert Ogden's brilliant (though I think finally unsuccessful) attempt to show that atheism is a logical impossibility. Atheism, Ogden asserts, "is not the absence of faith, but the presence of faith in the perverted form of idolatry."[35] Although I am perfectly happy to argue that atheism is not the truth about reality, I am surely not ready to affirm that it is simply a perverted form of faith in God. Such a response fails, it seems to me, to take seriously the full radicality of atheism's challenge to Christian faith, and the depth of our current cultural pluralism. Surely, a serious engagement in modern culture requires us to acknowledge at least the possibility that atheism may be the truth about reality. Thus the atheist cannot from the outset be considered a perverted or distorted theist, but must be counted an equal partner in a debate whose particular arguments for a nontheistic interpretation of reality and against theism need to be heard and refuted.

The ease with which the best contemporary theologians assert the essential religiousness of all human beings and argue against the very possibility of authentic forms of atheism is an indication that the full implications of the new pluralism are not yet apparent to most theologians. Though pluralism is a political and cultural reality, it is not, these theologians seek to argue, an ultimate religious reality; for in the depths of our humanity, in the religious root of our being, we are all one. That is a powerfully attractive sentiment, and it may even be a claim Christians are compelled to make on the basis of our doctrine of creation. But it is decidedly not a claim that can be successfully argued, as Tracy, Ogden, and others believe, as a necessarily true proposition on general philosophical grounds. The eternal covenant between human rationality and the Christian faith has been shattered by the new pluralism.

The quest for some common ground between Christian faith and secular culture and for some common good in which all persons can share is extraordinarily important. I have tried to argue, however, in these concluding reflections, that if Christian theology is to make a significant contribution to that quest, it must forgo its commitment to the eternal covenant and seek to engage its culture in a broader and more *ad hoc* fashion.[36] The end of the eternal covenant may mean the end of systematic theology as it has commonly been understood in the modern era. Radical pluralism calls into question any attempt to ground the meaning and truth of Christian beliefs in a systematic philosophy independent of the Christian faith. But there is another way available for contemporary theologians, the way pioneered by Karl Barth. I have sought to show that Barth's view of theological method implies no stark dichotomy between church and world or faith and culture, but seeks rather to engage the world of culture from within an integral vision of reality as formed by the Christian gospel.

The Christian gospel asserts that for all our apparent differences and conflicts, all human beings live in a single world reconciled to God by Jesus Christ. But we cannot discover that seamless universe by the exercise of our natural capacities, nor can we use our philosophical skills to demonstrate its wholeness. For now "we see through a glass darkly." But in the biblical narrative and its culminating event, Christ's death and resurrection, we catch a glimpse of the future that God has prepared for the entire cosmos, a glory not worth comparing to the sufferings of this present time. Until the consummation of that glory, we are called to witness in word and deed to that God who has raised Jesus from the dead and now sends the Spirit to the world. As Christians struggle to fulfill that vocation, we can, I believe, receive both instruction and support for our task from the theology of Karl Barth.

NOTES

1. Both Protestant and Catholic theologians have tended to group Barth with the "neoorthodox" movement. See, for example, Langdon Gilkey, *Naming*

the Whirlwind (Indianapolis: Bobbs-Merrill, 1969), 73–106, and David Tracy, *Blessed Rage for Order* (New York: Seabury Press, 1978), 27–31. Tracy treats Barth and the other "neoorthodox" theologians simply as "critical moments" in the history of modern liberalism.

2. The definitive work on the church in Nazi Germany is Klaus Scholder, *Die Kirchen und das Dritte Reich.* Band 1, *Vorgeschichte und Zeit der Illusionen, 1918–1934* (Frankfurt: Ullstein, 1977). This projected multi-volume work was not completed due to Professor Scholder's untimely death in 1985. The first German volume has been translated and published in two English volumes: *The Churches and the Third Reich.* Vol. 1: *1918–1934,* trans. (Philadelphia: Fortress Press, 1988) and *The Churches and the Third Reich.* Vol. 2: *The Year of Disillusionment, 1934: Barmen and Rome,* trans. John Bowden (Philadelphia: Fortress Press, 1988). Other studies in English of the churches' encounter with Nazism include J. S. Conway, *The Nazi Persecution of the Churches, 1933–1945* (London: Weidenfeld & Nicholson, 1968), and Ernst Helmreich, *The German Churches Under Hitler* (Detroit: Wayne State University Press, 1979). For works that focus primarily on Roman Catholicism's situation in the Third Reich, see Gordon Zahn, *German Catholics and Hitler's Wars* (New York: Sheed & Ward, 1962), and Günter Lewy, *The Catholic Church and Nazi Germany* (New York: McGraw-Hill, 1964).

3. Karl Barth, *Theologische Existenz Heute,* 1 (1933). English translation: *Theological Existence Today,* trans. R. Birch Hoyle (London: Hodder & Stoughton, 1933).

4. Karl Barth, "Erklärung uber das rechte Verständnis der reformatorischen Bekenntnisse in der Deutschen Evangelischen Kirche der Gegenwart," *Theologische Existenz Heute,* 7 (1943): 9–15.

5. Eberhard Busch, *Karl Barth: His Life from Letters and Autobiographical Texts,* trans. John Bowden (Philadelphia: Fortress Press, 1976), 245. There is some controversy about whether this event occurred precisely as Barth described it. It certainly could not have occurred on May 16, because that afternoon Barth took the 3:11 P.M. train from Frankfurt back to Bonn. Most likely, the famous "Lutheran siesta" took place on May 15. Helmut Traub recalls that Asmussen was overcome with an "acute migraine" and retired to his room after *Mittagessen* and that Breit received an urgent long-distance telephone call that occupied his time after the midday meal. Barth used that time to draft an initial version of the Barmen theses. Thus the event does not reflect quite so badly on the Lutheran participants as Barth's gleeful telling of the tale would imply. For a thorough reconstruction of the events of these days, see Martin Rohkramer, "Die Synode von Barmen in ihren zeitgeschichtlichen Zusammenhangen," *Bekennende Kirche wagen,* ed. Jürgen Moltmann (Munich: Chr. Kaiser Verlag, 1984), 34–41. See also Scholder, *The Churches and the Third Reich,* vol. 2, 136–137.

6. A thorough analysis of the events that led to the creation of the Lutheran Council has yet to be done. The best current accounts are Gerhard Niemoeller, *Die erste Bekenntnissynode der Deutschen Evangelische Kirche zu Barmen,* Band 1, *Geschichte, Kritik, und Bedeutung der Synode und ihrer theologischen Erklärung* (Göttingen: Vandenhoeck & Ruprecht, 1959), 188–229, and Scholder, *The Churches and the Third Reich,* vol. 2, 160–171.

7. *Die Bekenntnisse und grundsätzlichen Äeusserungen zur Kirchenfrage,* collected and introduced by Karl Dietrich Schmidt. Band 2 (Göttingen: Vandenhoeck & Ruprecht, 1935), 35.

8. Werner Elert, *Allgemeine Evangelisch-Lutherische Kirchenzeitung* 67 (June 29, 1934): 603.

9. Niemoeller, *Die erste Bekenntnissynode,* 151.

10. Ibid., 150.

11. Eberhard Bethge, "Troubled Self-Interpretation and Uncertain Reception in the Church Struggle, in *The German Church Struggle and the Holocaust,* eds. Franklin H. Littell and Hubert G. Locke (Detroit: Wayne State University Press, 1974), 177.

12. Arthur Cochrane, *The Church's Confession Under Hitler* (Philadelphia: Westminster Press, 1962), 197.

13. Langdon Gilkey, *Naming the Whirlwind* (Indianapolis: Bobbs-Merrill, 1969), 102–103.

14. Paul Althaus, *Evangelium und Leben: Gesammelte Vorträge* (Gutersloh: Verlag von C. Bertelsmann, 1927), 115. Quoted in James Zabel, *Nazism and the Pastors* (Missoula, Mont.: Scholars Press, 1976), 85.

15. Emanuel Hirsch, *Deutsches Volkstum und evangelischer Glaube* (Hamburg: Hanseatische Verlagsanstalt, 1934), 5. Quoted in Zabel, *Nazism and the Pastors,* 63.

16. Althaus, *Evangelium und Leben,* 97. Quoted in Zabel, *Nazism and the Pastors,* 63.

17. Van A. Harvey, *The Historian and the Believer* (New York: Macmillan, 1966), 157–158.

18. Friedrich Schleiermacher, *On the Glaubenlehre,* trans. James Duke and Francis Schüssler Fiorenza (Ann Arbor: Scholars Press, 1981), 61, 64.

19. Barth, *Theologische Existenz Heute,* 3. English translation: *Theological Existence Today,* 9.

20. Karl Barth, "Concluding Unscientific Postscript on Schleiermacher," in *Karl Barth: The Theology of Schleiermacher,* ed. Dietrich Ritschl (Grand Rapids: Eerdmans, 1982), 205.

21. Bill James, *The Bill James Baseball Abstract 1984* (New York: Ballantine Books, 1984), 9.

22. Karl Barth, "Lutherfeier," *Theologische Existenz Heute,* 4 (1933): 20.

23. Karl Barth, *Church Dogmatics,* vol. 1, pt. 1, *The Doctrine of the Word of God* (Edinburgh: T. & T. Clark, 1980), 295–383.

24. Karl Barth, "The Word of God and the Task of the Ministry," *The Word of God and the Word of Man,* trans. Douglas Horton (n.p.: Pilgrim Press, 1928), 186.

25. Tracy, *Blessed Rage for Order,* 106.

26. Karl Barth, "Schicksal und Idee in der Theologie," in *Theologische Fragen und Antworten* (Evangelischer Verlag, 1957). This passage is from George Hunsinger's typescript translation of this essay.

27. Karl Barth, *Evangelical Theology,* trans. Grover Foley (Grand Rapids: Eerdmans, 1963), 35.

28. Barth, "Schicksal und Idee in der Theologie," 9.

29. Robert Jenson, *Alpha and Omega: A Study in the Theology of Karl Barth* (New York: Thomas Nelson & Sons, 1963).

30. I have offered a critique of Barth on this matter and developed an alternative conception of revelation in *Theology and Revelation: The Gospel as Narrated Promise* (Notre Dame: University of Notre Dame Press, 1985)

31. Martin Luther, *Lectures on Galatians, 1535,* vol. 26 of *Luther's Works,* ed. Jaroslav Pelikan (St. Louis: Concordia, 1963), 64, 73.

32. Blaise Pascal, *Pensées,* trans. A. J. Krailsheimer (New York: Penguin Books, 1966), 152.

33. Alasdair MacIntyre, *After Virtue* (Notre Dame: University of Notre Dame Press, 1981).

34. Alasdair MacIntyre, *Whose Justice? Which Rationality?* (Notre Dame: University of Notre Dame Press, 1988).

35. Schubert Ogden, *The Reality of God* (New York: Harper & Row, 1963), 23.

36. For an example of such a procedure, see William Werpehowski, *"Ad hoc* Apologetics," *Journal of Religion,* 66, no. 3 (July 1986): 282–301.

5

I HAVE HEARD
THE CRY OF MY PEOPLE:
DISCERNING THE CALL OF GOD
IN THE CRIES OF GOD'S PEOPLE[1]

I

In the course of those many days the king of Egypt died. And the people of Israel groaned under their bondage, and cried out for help, and their cry under bondage came up to God. And God heard their groaning, and God remembered his covenant with Abraham, with Isaac, and with Jacob. And God saw the people of Israel, and God knew their condition. . . . Then the LORD said, "I have seen the affliction of my people who are in Egypt, and have heard their cry because of their taskmasters; I know their sufferings, and I have come down to deliver them out of the hand of the Egyptians, and to bring them up out of that land to a good and broad land, a land flowing with milk and honey."

(Ex. 2:23–25; 3:7–8)

Seen from space, the orb of the world appears to be a beautiful blue and white sphere delicately suspended against a black background. The astronauts who have experienced this sight firsthand tell us that the viewer is nearly overwhelmed by the awesome beauty and the silent serenity of the earth. In the airless void of space, no sound can be heard, and the visual splendor of this fragile globe communicates a sense of tranquillity and well-being.

As we leave the ethereal realms of space, however, and draw closer to this planet that is home to us all, that sense of tranquillity and well-being begins to dissipate. Approaching the upper ranges of the atmosphere, we discover that the ozone layer, the delicate envelope of gases that protects us from the killing effect of the sun's ultraviolet rays, has been depleted and that holes have developed in the polar regions, allowing lethal doses of energy to enter our environment. The cause? The desire of the world's affluent to have their local environments cooled and refrigerated; their deodorants, hair sprays, and insecticides propelled from aerosol cans; their drinks and fast-food sandwiches boxed in Styrofoam cartons. Meanwhile, the chlorofluorocarbons unleashed by these luxuries silently destroy the delicately balanced atmosphere that makes life itself possible.

As we penetrate the layers of the atmosphere, the beauty of God's creation is still evident. The brilliant blue of the refracted sunlight, the firmament of Genesis 1, embraces us as we hurtle toward the earth's surface. But as we draw nearer to the land, the unmistakable brown and gray haze of civilization, the industrial and chemical pollutants that befoul our air, becomes evident. And as we gaze upon the waters and the land—the land that "put forth vegetation, plants yielding seed, and fruit trees bearing fruit" (Gen. 1:11); the land that brought forth "living creatures according to their kinds: cattle and creeping things and beasts of the earth" (Gen. 1:24); the waters that brought forth "swarms of living creatures, . . . the great sea monsters and every living creature that moves, with which the waters swarm" (Gen. 1:20, 21)—we see God's good and fecund creation becoming a place of devastation and destruction.

We look in horror as global warming distorts rainfall patterns, extending the arid deserts of Africa into formerly inhabited places. Pictures of malnourished children with swollen bellies, of emaciated adults so weak that they cannot brush away the flies from their faces, of people dying by the thousands for lack of water to drink—these pictures will not soon leave our memories. In this beautiful land of Brazil, we see the devastation of the rain forests and the destruction of those cultures that have learned for centuries to coexist with the natural environment. The Amazon basin, one of the last places on earth where the land and waters literally teem and swarm with the manifold creatures of God's good creation, now faces destruction at the hands of those who would extract profit from pristine and fragile forests that provide an essential "green lung" for the entire earth. Inland waterways and harbors throughout the world have become so filthy that they can sustain virtually no life other than the green and red algae that feed off the fecal bacteria that proliferate in the otherwise dead waters. Boston harbor in my own hometown is little more than an open sewer, the victim of decades of chemical and sewage contamination.

"And God saw everything that [God] had made, and behold, it was very good" (Gen. 1:31). What has become of God's good creation, now that it has been in the charge of human stewards for these many millennia? How have we acquitted ourselves as stewards of the earth? How shall we account for our stewardship before the Lord of all creation? Will the apocalyptic judgment of the prophet Isaiah, uttered more than 2500 years ago, become reality in our time?

> The earth mourns and withers,
>   the world languishes and withers;
>   the heavens languish together with the earth.
> The earth lies polluted
>   under its inhabitants;
> for they have transgressed the laws,
>   violated the statutes,
>   broken the everlasting covenant.
> Therefore a curse devours the earth,
>   and its inhabitants suffer for their guilt;
> therefore the inhabitants of the earth are scorched,
>   and few men are left. . . .
> The earth is utterly broken,
>   the earth is rent asunder,
>   the earth is violently shaken.
> The earth staggers like a drunken man,
>   it sways like a hut;
> its transgression lies heavy upon it,
>   and it falls, and will not rise again.
>   (Isa. 24:4–6, 19–20)

We are surrounded by the cries of God's people in need. Some of these cries are vividly audible, like the cries of the Eastern Europeans who have recently attained the freedom they had demanded, or the cries of the poor and destitute in the streets of countless cities across the globe, people who struggle to keep their dignity despite being denied the most basic necessities of life. Other cries are inaudible or barely heard: those who have abandoned their hope and live lives of silent desperation; those who in illness or hunger or distress can simply echo the groaning of a creation in travail.

We do not have the luxury of the distant view of earth from space, where the airless void refuses to carry the world's cries of despair. We hear the cries all around us and wonder what we are being called to do about it all. We wonder where in these voices do we hear the call of God? And to what kind of action is God calling us through the cries of his people?

Since its earliest days, the Lutheran tradition has been associated with a tendency to separate religious and political matters, to keep justification and justice clearly distinct. According to Luther, the righteousness of faith must be clearly distinguished from civic righteousness if the purity of the gospel is to be maintained. The righteousness of faith is a pure gift of God mediated through the work of Christ. The transformation from unrighteousness to righteousness takes place through the declarative act of God in Christ; in that act, the sinner remains perfectly passive as God alone acts to justify. Civic righteousness, on the other hand, can be produced by the intentional activity of citizens, independent of their status before God. Luther was fond of saying that the Turks and heathen can produce the works of civic righteousness, but, he would quickly add, "The righteousness that justifies me before the civil judge is not to be identified with righteousness before God."

This fundamental distinction between the righteousness of faith and civic righteousness has made the problem of relating faith to political action particularly difficult among Lutherans. Some European and North American Lutherans have argued that the gospel bears no positive relation to the struggle for justice in the civic realm. At a 1985 consultation on this topic, held in Mexico City, Professor Gerhard Forde of Luther-Northwestern Seminary argued that "justification and justice cannot be put together by us in any sort of positive or artificial synthesis. It is like trying to make a positive synthesis between law and gospel, or between the old and the new age. Thus if one is to follow Luther's lead, the way ahead would seem to lie through negation rather than positive synthesis." By contrast, Lutheran theologians in Third World countries have sought to show the necessary interdependence between justification and justice. So at the same Mexico City conference, Dr. Victorio Araya of Costa Rica argued that "the condemned of the earth present to us in a radical and demanding way the question of the justice and justification of God."

The future of world Lutheranism, and Protestant Christianity in general, depends in large part on the way in which we understand the vocation and mission to which God is calling us in a world so desperately in need of the healing power of the gospel. We are, I believe, at a historic juncture in history. We have an opportunity to begin shaping the future of our common life as we look toward the twenty-first century. How do we respond to the cries of God's people, affirming our historic tradition, yet adapting to the demands of a world that "languishes and withers," an earth that "lies polluted under its inhabitants"? How do we, as Christians, hear the call of God in the midst of the cries of God's people?

II

Then the Lord said, . . . "Behold, the cry of the people of Israel has come to me, and I have seen the oppression with which the Egyptians oppress them. Come, I will send you to Pharaoh that you may bring forth my people, the children of Israel, out of Egypt." But Moses said to God, "Who am I that I should go to Pharaoh, and bring the children of Israel out of Egypt?"

(Ex. 3:7–11)

Any sensitive Christian today surely feels a bit like Moses. In numbing yet chilling detail, horrifying statistics depict the magnitude of the plight of God's suffering people: 500 million hungry, one billion living in extreme poverty, 40 million deaths a year from hunger and malnutrition, 1.5 billion without access to medical care, 2 billion without a stable water supply. And like Moses, each of us thinks, "Who am I that I should bear the responsibility for addressing this extraordinary situation? How can I, a person of privilege, a highly educated and reasonably wealthy American, possibly speak to a condition of suffering and deprivation that goes far beyond my own experience?" When faced with the enormity of human suffering, you, too, might ask with Moses, "But who am I?"

As you know, God was hardly daunted by Moses' self-effacing response. For each of Moses' excuses God had a more powerful reply, until finally Moses crumbled under the sheer weight of God's persistence. So, too, God will continue to pursue us until we heed God's call within the cries of God's people. But unlike Moses, we see no burning bush. We do not hear the voice of God calling us by name. We have no miraculous signs to reassure us of the presence of God. We have only the cries of God's people in their suffering and affliction, the groaning of the creation in travail—or so it sometimes seems. And that suffering and affliction, those cries and groanings can so overwhelm us that, like Moses, we want to run from the call of God. We want to stop our ears and find some peace and tranquillity, some place where we can restore our souls and our spirits. Opportunities abound in today's world to allow just such an escape from the cries of God's people. Some of these temptations to evasion are evident: the pursuit of material wealth and pleasures among the affluent; the momentary release that drugs provide young people—particularly those caught in the spiral of poverty and violence; the mindless involvement in the superficialities of popular culture. We think that these transitory diversions provide us happiness; in fact, they are futile attempts to escape our responsibility for a world in need.

Other temptations to evasion are more subtle and even come in religious garb. Various movements, flying the banner of "spirituality," beckon to us, inviting us to explore the interiority of our souls, to luxuriate in the good feelings of meditation and contemplation. Such spiritual exercises are not in and of themselves to be shunned, but if they direct us simply toward the self and away from our neighbors in need, then they are yet another expression of our fallenness, another example of the *incurvatus in se* that Augustine and Luther identified as the root of all sin. Diversions, whether material or spiritual, will not deflect our persistent God from calling us to respond to the cries of God's people.

But the question remains, How do we identify the call of God within the cacophony of cries we hear all around us? We must act without the guidance of a vision, or a divine voice, or a miraculous sign. How can we know if we are acting in accord with God's will for us and for God's people in need? How do we distinguish the call of God from the projections of our own hearts and imaginations? This question has always been most difficult for all Christians but especially for Lutherans to answer. Our theological heritage leads us to be cautious in identifying any action in history unambiguously with the action of God. Although we are confident that God is always present for us in the proclamation of the gospel and the administration of the sacraments, our keen sense of the fallibility and fallenness of creation keeps us from being equally confident in the realm of history and politics. The tragic events in Germany in the 1920s, 1930s, and 1940s demonstrate how difficult it is for Lutherans to avoid the extremes of political fanaticism on the one hand and political inaction on the other. Some Lutherans were willing to identify the hand of God in those forces that undermined the fragile democracy of the Weimar Republic, but few were able to hear the voice of God in the suffering of God's chosen people, the Jews. Somehow we must avoid a premature identification of God's call with our own most precious political programs, while remaining open to the genuine call of God in the voices of those who suffer. Do we have resources in the Lutheran tradition that can provide the guidance we need as we seek the voice of God in the voices of those who suffer?

III

And the people of Israel groaned under their bondage, and cried out for help, and their cry under bondage came up to God. And God heard their groaning, and God remembered his covenant with Abraham, with Isaac, and with Jacob.

(Ex. 2:23–24)

The central theological idea in this text is the notion of "covenant." If we truly grasp the biblical view of covenant, then we will come to see that there is no inherent conflict between justification and justice. If we genuinely understand the God of the covenant, then we will see that God's righteousness and God's justice are both manifestations of God's "steadfast love." By interpreting the Lutheran heritage in light of the biblical view of covenant, we will be enabled better to discern the call of God in the midst of the cries of God's people.

> Then Moses said to God, "If I come to the people of Israel and say to them, 'The God of your fathers has sent me to you,' and they ask me, 'What is his name?' what shall I say to them?" God said to Moses, ["I WILL BE WHAT I WILL BE."] And he said, "Say this to the people of Israel, ['I WILL BE] has sent me to you.' "

When Moses sought from God further clarification concerning God's identity, he received this puzzling opaque response. To this very day, scholars are uncertain how to translate the name that God reveals to Moses. Pious Jews will not even speak the name; they simply write the four letters YHWH. Christians have recently developed the custom of speaking the name Yahweh, but we are still uncertain what the name means. I have used one common translation, "I WILL BE WHAT I WILL BE," because it captures both the ambiguity and the future orientation of God's reality. God cannot and will not be known by such a simple device as a name. The name Yahweh is designed to be ambiguous. It requires those who believe to seek further if they wish to discover the identity of this God. It requires the one who would hear the call of God to look at the actions that God performs in the world. We, like Moses, are told to look to God's actions if we want to hear the call of God in the midst of the cries of God's people. If you want to know this God, look at the deeds God has performed.

Those deeds cluster around the central concept of the Exodus text, the covenant. God remembers the covenant made with Abraham, Isaac, and Jacob, and so acts to deliver them from bondage in Egypt. Just as God called Abraham and Sarah out of the land of Haran and promised to give to them and their descendants a new land as "an everlasting possession," so now God calls this people out of Egypt in order to bring them back to the land of promise: "And I will establish my covenant between me and you and your descendants after you throughout their generations for an everlasting covenant, to be God to you and to your descendants after you" (Gen. 17:7). God's call is thus linked to the making and remembering of an everlasting promise, and God's act of deliverance is an act of faithfulness to that promise. The exodus is a liberating act by a God who is faithful to the covenant, faithful to the everlasting promise. This act of justice proceeds from a God who is identified by covenant faithfulness.

This identification of God through his covenanted actions is made even clearer in the giving of the law at Sinai. There God once more links the divine name with covenant faithfulness: "YHWH passed before [Moses], and proclaimed, 'YHWH, YHWH, a God merciful and gracious, slow to anger, and abounding in steadfast love and faithfulness' " (Ex. 34:6). The call to Abraham and Sarah, the liberation from bondage in Egypt, the giving of the law at Sinai—all these must be understood as actions that proceed from God's identity as the God of the covenant. These actions are thus manifestations of God's mercy, grace, steadfast love, and faithfulness. As Moses tells the people of Israel before they enter into the Promised Land, "Because [God] loved your [forebears] and chose their descendants after them, [God] brought you out of Egypt with his own presence, by his great power" (Deut. 4:37). God's act of liberation is an expression of God's steadfast love and faithfulness.

If there is a single word most often associated with God's faithfulness to the promise, it is the word "steadfast love," *hesed*. Indeed, if we are to understand the biblical notion of justice, we need to see it as an expression of the steadfast love that characterizes the covenant relationship. Hear the words of the prophet Isaiah:

> "Give counsel, grant justice; . . . hide the outcasts, betray not the fugitive. . . . When the oppressor is no more, and destruction has ceased, and he who tramples under foot has vanished from the land, then a throne will be established in steadfast love and on it will sit in faithfulness in the tent of David one who judges and seeks justice and is swift to do righteousness."
>
> (Isa. 16:3–5)

The righteous judge, the one who genuinely seeks justice, is the one who is faithful to the covenant and whose action is an expression of steadfast love. Therefore those who are in covenant relation with the righteous God must guide their actions by the same covenant standard. Genuine justice proceeds from our faithful recognition of God's undeserved mercy toward us. God's justice is an expression of God's willingness to remain faithful to the covenant, even when we have failed to keep our part of the bargain. When God heard the cries of this people in bondage, God simply "remembered this covenant" and "came down to deliver them out of the hands of the Egyptians." God did not first inquire concerning the degree and quality of their faithfulness; rather, their cries were sufficient to remind God of the covenant, and God acted out of steadfast love and faithfulness. Genuine justice proceeds from our faithful recognition of God's steadfast love toward us. That is why the prophet Micah chooses covenant language to remind the people of Israel about their responsibilities for justice: "[God] has showed you, O man, what is good; and what does the LORD require of you but to do justice, and to [desire steadfast love] (*hesed*), and to walk humbly with your God" (Micah 6:8).

The other primary term used in the Old Testament to identify God as God of the covenant is righteousness, *sedeqa*. Listen again to the words of the prophet Isaiah: "When the oppressor is no more, and destruction has ceased, and he who tramples under foot has vanished from the land, then a throne will be established in steadfast love and on it will sit in faithfulness in the tent of David one who judges and seeks justice and is swift to do righteousness" (Isa. 16:4–5). In this passage, the basic notions of covenant theology come together: steadfast love, faithfulness, righteousness, and justice. It is particularly important for our purposes to note that righteousness and justice are closely linked with God's steadfast love and faithfulness. "Righteousness" is the term that describes God's steadfast love and faithfulness in relation to the covenant partner. God's righteousness is revealed when God acts in love to confirm and fulfill the promises God has made in the covenant. Justice is accomplished when the promises of the covenant are fulfilled. Therefore, if we want to know what God is calling us to do when we hear the cries of God's people, we must look to the promises God has made to us in the covenant.

In order to understand the full extent of those promises, we must, of course, look to the one in whom all the promises of God are fulfilled— Jesus Christ, for Jesus Christ is the righteousness of God; Jesus Christ is the ultimate expression of God's steadfast love and faithfulness. The great achievement of the apostle Paul, an achievement Lutherans all too often fail to grasp, is that he brought together the Jewish covenant theology of righteousness with the unique revelation in Jesus Christ. When Paul speaks of the righteousness of God in the book of Romans, he presupposes the great covenant theology of Judaism. Luther's great insight into the gospel, gleaned from the book of Romans, took place as he struggled with the notion of God's righteousness. When Luther finally realized that God's righteousness was the power by which God makes us righteous— that is, when he understood that God's righteousness is an expression of God's steadfast love and faithfulness—the gospel was revealed to him in all its majesty and wonder.

The challenge now before the contemporary Lutheran communion and all other Christian bodies is to extend that evangelical insight into our thinking about justice. If for the prophets justice is the extension of God's righteousness into the world, then we must ask ourselves how Jesus Christ, the righteousness of God, calls us to a ministry of justice in behalf of those who suffer. If we can discern the promises of God in Jesus Christ in behalf of those who suffer, we will begin to understand the call of God to us in the midst of cries of God's people.

IV

And as he sat at table, . . . behold, many tax collectors and sinners came and sat down with Jesus and his disciples. And when the Pharisees saw this, they said to his disciples, "Why does your teacher eat with tax collectors and sinners?" But when he heard it, he said, "Those who are well have no need of a physician, but those who are sick. Go and learn what this means, 'I desire [steadfast love], and not sacrifice.' For I came not to call the righteous, but sinners."

(Matt. 9:10–13; cf. Mark 2:13–17 and Luke 5:27–32)

As we turn our attention to the life, ministry, death, and resurrection of Jesus, we begin to see even more clearly the close connection between justice and God's steadfast love. In entering the world of the New Testament, however, we must reckon with another concept that is central to our understanding of God's covenant faithfulness, the concept of sin. In the first chapter of the Gospel of Matthew, Joseph is visited by an angel who reassures him that the child Mary carries is "of the Holy Spirit. She will bear a son," the angel announces, "and you shall call his name Jesus, for he will save his people from their sins" (Matt. 1:20–21). The Gospel writer is reflecting a popular etymology of the name Jesus or, in its Hebrew equivalent, Joshua, in which the name means "Yahweh is salvation." Thus the very name of Jesus is connected with the God of Israel, the righteous God who shows steadfast love in faithfulness to the covenant. Jesus is thus identified as Yahweh's agent of salvation, the one who "will save his people from their sins."

We must exercise great care in interpreting the notion of sin in the New Testament. We have been influenced by centuries of interpretation in which the concept of sin has become increasingly narrowed and personalized. We are apt to think of sin primarily in moral terms, as those acts of commission or omission by which we become guilty in the sight of God. The Gospel writers, however, have a much broader and more inclusive understanding of sin. For them a sinner is one who stands on the margins, one who is an outcast from the primary society, one who is vulnerable because of lack of health, or social standing, or economic status. Among the many terms included in the category of "sinner" within the Gospels are the following: tax collectors, the sick and infirm, the poor, the ritually unclean, those who hunger and thirst, those who are persecuted for righteousness sake, those who mourn, those possessed by demons, the naked, the strangers, the prisoners, "the least of these," our brothers and sisters. I realize that my suggestion that all these persons belong in the category "sinner" may be both surprising and controversial, but I believe a close reading of the Gospel narratives will confirm this interpretation. A sinner, in the Gospel texts, is one who has been rejected and marginalized, one who appears to be outside the protective care of God's covenant steadfast love.

This broad use of the term *sin* in no way suggests that those who are on the margins are morally responsible for their plight. Quite the contrary. As Jesus' reply to the disciples concerning the man who was born blind makes perfectly clear, those who suffer misfortune do so through no fault of their own. Blindness, ritual impurity, poverty, disease—these unhappy circumstances of life ought not lead to the shunning or rejection of those who fall victim to them. These conditions lead to marginal status solely because society consigns such persons to the margins. The self-appointed righteous ones designate those who suffer as "sinners." And it is precisely to such sinners—for their salvation—that Jesus is sent. He does not reject the term by which society identifies these outcasts; rather, he identifies with that term and those who bear it, and thereby redeems them. Herein lies the mystery of the gospel: that Jesus, the righteous one of God, identifies fully with sinners and outcasts, and thereby makes them righteous in God's sight. This is what Luther called that "blessed exchange" whereby Jesus becomes a sinner so that sinners might become righteous.[2]

In announcing the name of this child of Mary, the angel reveals that Jesus will be the "salvation of Yahweh," the agent of the righteous God who will extend God's steadfast covenant love to all sinners. The one who at his birth is identified with the righteous God then embarks on a ministry in which he becomes identified, not with the righteous, but with sinners: "For I came not to call the righteous but sinners." His table fellowship with tax collectors, prostitutes, lepers, and others who were ritually unclean is the tangible sign that the righteous one of God has identified himself with those who are thought to lie outside the sphere of God's steadfast love. But in identifying with those who are called "sinners," Jesus extends that steadfast love to them. Thus, to his detractors he quotes the passage from the prophet Amos, "Go and learn what this means, 'I desire steadfast love and not sacrifice.'" And that steadfast love ultimately extends to include the very fate that all sinners must suffer, the fate of exclusion from the gracious covenant of God. When from the cross Jesus utters that horrifying cry, "My God, my God, why have you forsaken me?" he speaks on behalf of all sinners, all those who, without his mission of mercy, would have been separated from the steadfast love of God. But in having accomplished that mission, Jesus fulfills the promise of Yahweh the God of Israel, that in Jesus God's people will find their salvation. By raising Jesus from the dead, God testifies that the mission of this prophet from Nazareth is God's own mission. Through Jesus, God's steadfast love is extended to include all persons, indeed, is extended to the entire world (see Matt. 26:13). As the Gospel narrative draws to a close, Jesus sends all those who would be disciples on a mission of steadfast love to "all nations." And the Gospel concludes, not surprisingly, with a final word of promise, a reminder that the one who at his birth was called "Immanuel, God with us" will now be with us "always, to the close of the age" (Matt. 28:20). Thus the righteous one of God promises that God's steadfast love will encompass all of space and time.

V

Return with me, if you will, to the picture with which I began, the picture of the fragile blue orb of the earth suspended against the ebony darkness of space. We have now seen the devastation visited upon this planet by human exploitation; we have smelled the putrid aromas generated by chemical wastes, sewage, and the terrible burning of the rain forests; we have touched and been touched by the sufferings of those enslaved by poverty, disease, and political tyranny; we have heard the incessant cries of God's people in need. Our senses have been attuned to a creation groaning in travail, and we know that within these cries and groanings we have heard the call of God. Like Moses, we must now respond to that call and take up the responsibilities God has given us.

Our study of the Bible's covenant theology has helped us identify the God who is calling to us from within the cries of God's people: Yahweh, Creator of the universe, God of the covenant, the one revealed in Jesus Christ. This is the God who has created "an everlasting covenant" with "all flesh that is upon the earth" (Gen. 9:17). This is the God who called Abraham and Sarah to be the parents of a people of promise. This is the God who heard the cries of those people in bondage, remembered the covenant, and came down to deliver this people from slavery. Yahweh is the God who chose Jesus of Nazareth to be the agent of salvation, the one who will extend God's steadfast love to the whole world. Yahweh, the one who called to Moses out of the burning bush, now calls to us from his beautiful yet broken creation. Yahweh remains "I will be who I will be": the righteous one, the God of steadfast love, the God who is faithful to the covenant. If we look carefully at these three characteristics of our calling God, then we will begin to discern the actions to which we are called.

> [God] has showed you . . . what is good; and what does the LORD require of you but to do justice, and to [desire steadfast love,] and to walk humbly with your God?"
>
> (Micah 6:8)

"... *to do justice.*" As people of the covenant, as those who have experienced the steadfast love of our righteous God, we are now called to a ministry of justice in behalf of those who live on the margins, those who are the outcasts of our societies, those who suffer oppression. As disciples of the crucified and risen Christ, we have a special responsibility to extend God's covenant protection to those who are vulnerable and powerless. Cruciform discipleship calls us to identify with the plight of those who suffer innocently, "the least of these," our brothers and sisters. But that identification brings with it a responsibility to proclaim the good news that the crucified has risen, that God's justice and mercy extend to the whole world. People of the covenant are people of promise, people who witness to a cruciform hope within a world of needless suffering.

Doing justice is a complicated matter in today's world, and we must beware of seizing simple solutions to complex problems. There is no "quick fix" for the myriad pains of a groaning creation. In responding to the cries of God's people, we need to develop diverse approaches to questions of justice. In some situations, our role should be that of the prophet, holding up a vision of God's righteousness and condemning those who subject God's people to oppression. In other contexts, where the injustices are less clear and more subtle, we may have to engage in serious attempts to study problems, to gain knowledge about political and economic systems, and encourage long-range programs of reform and modification. In still other circumstances, we may have to act decisively to rescue those who are victims of injustice but have no one to speak for them or to act in their behalf. If we are to be agents of our righteous God, seeking to establish peace with justice, then we must be open to the many and often surprising ways in which our God acts to deliver people from bondage.

Over the last few years, we have seen freedom movements develop in the Philippines, in China, throughout Eastern Europe, and in Africa and Latin America. Although these movements have sought political and economic freedom for their people, they have been strikingly diverse in approach and strategy. We should expect nothing less from a world as wonderfully complex as the one created by our righteous God. As people of the covenant, we need to keep our approaches to justice flexible, even as we continue to witness to the righteousness of our loving God.

" . . . and to desire steadfast love." As we saw in our study of covenant theology, justice proceeds from the steadfast love of our righteous God. Justice is the form that God's steadfast love takes in relation to those who suffer in the world. For people of the covenant, the search for justice must always proceed from that steadfast love by which God has reconciled the world. Indeed, justice must be understood as the extension of God's steadfast love to those who are most vulnerable and defenseless.

In order to be effective agents of justice in the world, it is essential that we maintain a clear identity as people of the covenant, that community gathered in the presence of the crucified and risen Christ. Therefore we must seek in our worship, in our Christian education, and in our mission to the world to be that distinctive community of the baptized, commissioned to extend the steadfast love of God to the whole world. Just as we struggle to recognize and confess the identity of the God who calls us to covenant faithfulness, so also we must struggle with our own identity as disciples of the crucified and risen Christ. Part of that struggle will include the question of how we are to organize ourselves as a world communion of Christians. If that discussion is to be more than a political and politicized argument among interest groups, we must keep clearly before our eyes our calling to be a communion in service to the world, a communion of the reconciled seeking to extend God's steadfast love to the world. Our organizational structures must be designed to allow us maximum flexibility in responding to the myriad cries among God's people in the world. And our discussion of this topic must itself manifest the qualities of steadfast love in our relations to one another. If we cannot be a community of love to one another, it is doubtful that we can be such a community for those in need in the world.

" . . . and to walk humbly with your God." The most extraordinary characteristic exhibited in the story of God's relation to the covenant people is the remarkable tenacity God shows in remaining faithful to promises. No matter how faithless, disobedient, or rebellious the covenant people become, God's love remains steadfast; God's promises remain secure. Yahweh, "I will be who I will be," is a God of memory and hope, a God who will always remember the covenant and thus invites us to enter God's future with confidence. God's faithfulness to the covenant is our greatest comfort and hope as we seek to respond to the cries of those who are in need.

Because we know that God will remain faithful to the promises, we are liberated from the devastating fear that the accomplishment of justice in the world depends solely upon our efforts. The primacy and priority of God's grace frees us from the self-defeating effort of seeking our salvation in the quest for justice. Because our salvation has been secured by Christ's death and resurrection, we are now free to seek justice for the neighbor in need. At this essential point, it is proper to distinguish (though not to separate) justification and justice. We seek justice freely, because we have been freely justified. We seek to be a communion of steadfast love, because we are the recipients of God's steadfast love. We seek to be faithful covenant partners, because God's faithfulness will endure forever.

Because God has promised to be "with [us] always, until the close of the age," we can become genuine people of hope, a communion that exemplifies the cruciform hope of the gospel. As people of hope, we are committed to the struggle for justice "for the long haul." For the church, the pursuit of justice is neither a transitory commitment to be forgotten when the next new cause beckons nor a desperate attempt at individual or corporate self-justification. Rather, the pursuit of justice is the form of life appropriate to those who have been justified by the crucified and risen Christ; it is the fitting expression of God's steadfast love in and for the world, because in Christ God's covenant love has been expanded to include the whole of the universe, for salvation has been promised not only to the human creatures of God's creation but to the whole of creation itself. Thus we wait in hope for a liberated creation.

We are surrounded by the cries of a creation "groaning in travail"; but as people of the covenant, we must also proclaim that "the creation itself will be set free from its bondage to decay and obtain the glorious liberty of the children of God" (Rom. 8:21). To depict the cries and groanings alone is to preach a gospel of death without resurrection. To proclaim a message of liberty without a genuine sense of the suffering and bondage from which the creation must be freed is to substitute a gospel of optimism for the cruciform hope of the Christian gospel. In Christ we have glimpsed a future in which God's steadfast love reigns eternally; in Christ we have been called to be witnesses in word and deed to that future. In Christ we are empowered once more to see the beautiful but battered orb of the world and to marvel that it and we remain beloved of God. In Christ we are enabled to join our hearts and voices to the words of the psalmist, words that might become the common prayer of all Christians: "Let thy steadfast love, O LORD, be upon us, even as we hope in thee" (Ps. 33:22).

NOTES

1. This chapter is adapted from my keynote address to the 1990 Lutheran World Federation Assembly in Curitiba, Brazil.

2. I do not want to give the impression that this discussion of sin and sinners in Matthew can be the basis for a complete doctrine of sin. Rather, I would argue that in those traditions that have for so long interpreted Paul's teaching on sin through the lens of Reformation teaching, the Gospel's emphasis on sin as marginality provides a counterpoint that must be integrated into the church's overall doctrine of sin and fallenness. As I have argued regarding Paul's notion of righteousness, a reconsideration of Jewish covenant theology would provide an essential first step in the reconstruction of the doctrine of sin.

6

WORSHIP AND
PUBLIC RESPONSIBILITY

LITURGY AND PUBLIC RESPONSIBILITY:
TWO EXAMPLES

In the German parliamentary elections of 1932, Adolf Hitler and his National Socialist Party gained the highest percentage of the national vote they were ever to receive in a free German election. This victory was the culmination of eighteen months of feverish and often violent campaigning during which the Nazi platform of *Blut und Boden*—the exaltation of loyalty to race, nation, and leader—became a fixture within German politics. The election result was hardly surprising, because by the end of the year 1931, the "cult of the Führer" had taken root in the fabric of Weimar Germany, and the road that would lead Hitler to the chancellery in Berlin had been established.

In the same year of 1931, in a small Benedictine Abbey at Maria Laach, in the heart of the vineyards of the Rhine valley, Abbot Ildefons Herwegen founded the Institute of Liturgical and Monastic Studies, thereby providing a teaching and scholarly focus to the liturgical movement that had been born at the same abbey seventeen years earlier. To the casual observer, these two events of 1931 would seem to be totally unrelated. Indeed, the founding of the institute could easily be seen as a typical religious escape from the exciting political events of the day, a time identified by the Lutheran theologian Paul Althaus as the "German hour" of decision. But only a superficial reading of these events would see them as disconnected, for in his lecture given at the founding of the institute on the theme "the nature of religious art," Dom Ildefons spoke the following words:

Religious art must, by its very nature, be social art. That is, it must grow out of the common faith, thought, experience, life, and not least of all, the common worship of the Church. The individuality of the artistic personality cannot, therefore, be its norm. The . . . norms of the community must come first . . . [No matter] how highly the individuality of the artist and of the nation are valued, they must . . . remain subordinate to the . . . norms of the religious community.[1]

For those with "ears to hear," the inherent criticism of the Nazi "cult of personality and nation" could hardly be clearer. At a time when the whole of German society was being politicized, this emphasis upon the primacy of the norms of Christian worship was a courageous political act.

At his Confessing Church seminary, established first at Zingst, Germany, in 1935, Dietrich Bonhoeffer created a community organized around serious spiritual discipline. Each day began with a service of readings, hymns, and prayers that was followed by a half-hour of silent meditation—all before breakfast! Although the seminary was criticized, even within the Confessing Church, for its so-called Catholic practices and radical fanaticism, Bonhoeffer remained convinced that only such a disciplined spiritual life would prepare his ordinands for the rigors of ministry in the Third Reich. As his biographer Eberhard Bethge tells us, "Bonhoeffer always made it absolutely clear that [this spiritual discipline] in no way represented a withdrawal from decisions in church politics, but rather a way of preparing to meet them."[2]

LITURGY AND PUBLIC RESPONSIBILITY: TWO PROPOSALS

These examples from a time and place so clearly removed from our current situation in the United States in the early 1990s serve as reminders of the deep relation between liturgy and public responsibility. Such examples illustrate a reality inherent in the very etymology of the word *leitourgia*, a Greek noun meaning "the discharge of a public office." In the context of the Greek *polis, leitourgia* involved engaging in public office at one's own expense, thereby offering service to the state and so contributing to the well-being of the community or *koinonia*. The language adopted by the early Christian community for its own worship life was clearly and explicitly public or political language.

But any act of adoption is simultaneously an act of transformation; thus the *leitourgia* offered in the context of the *koinonia tou Christou* is not service to the state and state's gods but service to and for Jesus Christ. But does that service have implications for the public world beyond the

113

borders of the Christian community? Does the service of *leitourgia* extend to the broader society, or is it primarily or even solely directed to the ecclesial community? Is Christian worship in any sense a *political* act?

In an essay entitled "Praying and Doing Justice," Paul Lehmann set forth the thesis that "politics are the business of liturgy." Arguing out of the Reformed tradition's close association of faith with obedience, Lehmann asserts that proper worship always has as its goal the accomplishment of justice in the world. The righteousness of faith must result in transformative justice within the public realm. Thus Christian worship is essentially political, and the *leitourgia* of the church extends naturally and directly into political action. "Praying without doing justly," Lehmann writes, "unmasks the integrity of Christian faith and obedience as disingenuous. Apart from doing justly, praying is narcissistic."[3]

In sharp contrast to Lehmann's position, Stanley Hauerwas has argued that "Christians must again understand that their first task is not to make the world better or more just. . . . Christians [must] rediscover that their most important social task is nothing less than to be a community capable of hearing the story of God we find in the scripture and living in a manner that is faithful to that story."[4] Adopting a position characteristic of the Anabaptist tradition, Hauerwas urges the church to think of itself as a "separated community." "The challenge," he writes, "is always for the church to be a 'contrast model' for all politics that know not God."[5] By being faithful to the narratives that shape Christian character, the church will witness to a way of life that stands apart from and in criticism of our liberal secular culture. Christian worship, then, must be an end in itself directed solely toward the cultivation of those peculiar theological virtues that mark the church as a distinctive community.

THE CHALLENGE TO NORTH AMERICAN CHRISTIANS

I want to suggest that neither of the positions I have just summarized provides us with the theological resources we need to face the distinctive challenge presented to North American Christians. Neither the politicalization of worship nor its sectarian separation from public life will suffice in our current situation. We must engage in a basic rethinking of the very categories by which we understand the church's relation to public life. We must find a middle way between the reduction of the Christian gospel to a program of political action and the isolation of that gospel from all political engagement.

It is undoubtedly ironic that I, dean of a theological school long identified with the liberal Protestant tradition, should be the one to bring you this particular message. For the ten years prior to coming to Harvard I was a member of the faculty of Haverford College, an institution founded and governed by the Society of Friends. These are two unlikely institutional affiliations for one who was born and raised a Lutheran (a Missouri Synod Lutheran, no less!), ordained into the Lutheran ministry, and now serves as active member on the clergy roster of the new Evangelical Lutheran Church in America. Perhaps it is even more unlikely that a theologian with my particular pedigree would seek to instruct others on the relation between liturgy and public responsibility, for, as I have indicated, the Lutheran tradition is not at its best on the question of Christian political responsibility. The Lutheran emphasis on the distinction between law and gospel demands (in contrast to the Reformed position already described) that the righteousness of faith be clearly and sharply distinguished from civic righteousness. The word and sacraments are "means of the Spirit" designed to mediate God's justifying grace to the sinner. To focus one's attention on the political effects of grace is to risk confusion of faith and works and thereby to lose the assurance of the gospel. The transformation from unrighteousness to righteousness takes place through the declarative act of God in Christ through word and sacrament. In that act, the sinner remains perfectly passive as God alone acts to justify. In order to preserve the Pauline sense that faith is "a gift of God not of works, lest anyone should boast," Luther denied that faith is in any sense "our doing."

For Luther, and for much of the Lutheran tradition as well, worship, the proclamation of the gospel and the administration of the sacraments, has been sharply and clearly distinguished from political activity in order to preserve the distinction between the righteousness of faith and civic righteousness. In his greater Galatians commentary, Luther makes the point quite clearly:

> Christians do not become righteous by doing righteous works; but once they have been justified by faith in Christ, they do righteous works. In civil life the situation is different; here one becomes a doer on the basis of deed, just as one becomes a lutenist by often playing the lute, as Aristotle says. But in theology one does not become a doer on the basis of works of the law; first there must be the doer, and then the deeds follow.[6]

The ironic implication in this argument is that if you would have good deeds done, then you must produce good doers. But good doers are not produced by attending to their doing; indeed, if you attend to doing, then you will be doomed to unrighteousness. True righteousness and the deeds that flow from it can only be produced by the justifying act of God in which the sinner remains purely passive. Politics must be kept out of worship if true righteousness is to prevail.

Not only is this position ironic; it has also had disastrous practical consequences throughout the history of Lutheranism. Gerald Strauss, in his book *Luther's House of Learning,* describes how difficult it became for Lutheran educators in the sixteenth and seventeenth centuries to "forge a motivational link" between faith's inner passive spirit and the external practices needed to form a public community of virtue. Why should Christians engage in the discipline of moral education when such efforts could not effect the central transformation of the self from *peccator* to *iustus?* Early Lutheran efforts to imbue those "habits of the heart" characteristic of good Christian citizens were finally undermined by their theological ambivalence about whether such efforts could possibly succeed. Strauss makes the point quite clearly: "Torn between their trust in the molding power of education and their admission that the alteration of men's nature was a task beyond human strength, [Lutheran educators] strove for success in their endeavors while conceding the likelihood of defeat."[7] The history of Lutheranism in subsequent centuries points to the terrible consequences of this paralysis concerning the public virtues of civic righteousness.

The challenge facing Christians in North America today is daunting indeed. We face a public world politically and morally fragmented by the strident debates over matters of public policy. Decision making in the public sphere increasingly lies in the hands of professionals who consider analytical precision, efficiency, and cost-effectiveness to be the ultimate criteria for policy formation. Considerations of equity, justice, and the public good are conspicuously absent from the deliberations of policymakers in business, government, and the professions. How can Christian churches expect to be heard within this complex pluralistic atmosphere? How can Christian theologians contribute to the conversation concerning the future of American public life?

AMERICAN PUBLIC LIFE:
THE CHALLENGE OF PLURALISM

Before we can consider the role that Christians might play in the current public debates, we need to have at least a rough-hewn understanding of the nature of public life in the United States today. Rather than attempt a general description of some features of our public culture, I want to focus on a single aspect of public life, the phenomenon identified by the current buzzword *pluralism.*

The heterogeneity of American life can be variously identified: our pluralism is ethnic, political, cultural, religious, and moral. We are distinguished by gender, race, class, and ethnic origin. Our cultural and ethnic diversity is in large part the result of those successive waves of immigrants who reached our shores throughout the nineteenth and twentieth centuries. The process of "Americanization" by which these immigrants were socialized into our common cultural heritage has been carefully described by contemporary sociologists. We described ourselves as the "melting pot" of the world, thereby emphasizing the homogeneity that emerged from the rich mixture of ethnic identities. We referred proudly to the "hyphenated Americans," those who combined their European or Asian heritage with their new American identity.

But during the past thirty years, the mythology of the melting pot has collided rudely with the reality of an unequal America. We realized that images of homogenization did not apply to those people who had come to our shores not by their own act of willing immigration but by our act of enslavement. During the remarkable years that began with the Supreme Court decision in *Brown v. Board of Education* and ended with the Kerner Commission report on civil disorders, the phrase "separate and unequal" was seared into the public consciousness. Despite the important advances made during the civil rights movement, the blue-ribbon panel that gathered in the aftermath of the riots of 1967 drew the "basic conclusion" that not only our educational system but our entire society was "separate and unequal." The melting pot seemed incapable of fusing those metals forged by the divisions of race and class.

The succeeding two decades have witnessed some important advances in race relations in the United States. Increasing numbers of African Americans have begun to achieve middle-class status and are enjoying the associated financial and social advantages. Racism, of course, remains an endemic problem in American culture, but it would be foolish not to recognize genuine progress when it occurs. Tragically, however, this success has been accompanied by an equally vexing problem—the emergence of "the underclass," a new, terribly disadvantaged group, predominantly black, caught in a deep spiral of poverty, drug addiction, and hopelessness in pockets of deprivation within our American cities. This phenomenon, so carefully and shockingly documented by the sociologist

William Julius Wilson, has created an even greater gap between power and privilege, wealth and well-being.[8]

During the 1970s and 1980s new issues of diversity have come to dominate our attention—those associated with gender discrimination. Although the churches of European origin could decry the racial inequality in our nation and even join in positive action to overcome it, their internal structures were essentially untouched by the battles over racism. This was not so with issues of gender. Now the churches were directly implicated in matters of discrimination; indeed, they became the battleground for some of the most important skirmishes. Questions of women's ordination, inclusive language, and power sharing within the church have given traditional ecclesiastical structures a good hard shake. The church itself—its hierarchical structure, its male priesthood and ministry, its male-dominated language—has been identified as the oppressor. Moreover, these ecclesiastical and theological failures have been linked with deeper and more frightening social patterns, particularly the shocking prevalence in our society of violence against women—verbal, physical, and sexual abuse.

We are as a nation and as churches seeking to come to terms with these profound social problems. And somehow the words *pluralism* and *diversity* seem insufficient to capture the social reality of those caught in the spiral of poverty or those psychologically and physically disabled by abuse. Insofar as the divisions of race, class, and gender manifest themselves in the life of the church, they are rooted in social problems that are part of our common public life. In this sense, then, the church and its worship life are profoundly linked to matters of public responsibility.

THE CHALLENGE OF PLURALISM:
SOME PROFFERED SOLUTIONS

Though the social problems I have just described are widely recognized, we can hardly be encouraged by the character of the current discussion of these issues. We face significant national problems—homelessness, poverty, drug abuse, domestic violence, AIDS; and yet the "hot topic" of the 1988 presidential campaign was the issue of whether American school children should recite the Pledge of Allegiance. Serious ethical problems need to be addressed in the economy, in our military and diplomatic systems, in the health care community, in the legal profession, and in the environment; yet we have no clear indication that politicians are willing to tackle these complicated issues in the current pluralistic political atmosphere.

The dizzying diversity of contemporary culture has created a climate in which many people are sorely tempted to withdraw from involvement in public life. They recognize the profundity of our cultural differences, despair of all attempts to adjudicate those disagreements, and so, weary of the strident public debates, retreat to private enclaves of like-minded persons. Those who succumb to this temptation implicitly or explicitly deny that there can be any meaningful public life; consequently, they seek to cultivate a few precious values that might endure within homogeneous communities separated from the public world. From time to time, representatives of these communities might emerge to offer their cynical observations on contemporary life, but they can imagine no constructive public contribution emerging from their separated communities.

This response to cultural pluralism can be found along the entire political spectrum within American life today. In conservative or neoconservative circles, it is often joined by a nostalgic longing for an imagined past of cultural homogeneity. Among radical progressives, it is most often linked to a utopian vision of a world that is possible only through revolutionary change. Those with liberal proclivities appear hard-pressed to articulate any vision at all for public life and are increasingly attracted to private dreams of personal happiness and security.

But all versions of the strategy of withdrawal fail to do justice to the complexity of the Christian gospel. Those who despair of any meaningful public life fail to recognize the enduring presence of God's creative hand in the public realm. In so doing, they rob the world of that theological virtue most needed in American public life—the virtue of hope. Grumpy cultural pessimists prefer nostalgia to Christian hope; angry cultural radicals confuse utopian dreams with the cruciform hope of the gospel; tired liberals abandon hope altogether, preferring the suffocating privacy of individual aspirations. But none of these responses offers an appropriate Christian engagement with the reality of pluralism, for all assume that our differences are so profound that we cannot work together for some common human good. All have abandoned the hope that we can forge a political community in which genuine disagreement and genuine conviction can coexist.

WORSHIP AND PUBLIC RESPONSIBILITY: A THEOLOGICAL PROPOSAL

Another way of describing the current crisis in public life is to say that we have lost a living sense of citizenship. Many Americans have become alienated from political activity, because they have no sense of belonging to a community of diverse persons dedicated to a common good. Government appears to be a huge, faceless bureaucracy unresponsive to the needs of citizens. The political process is apparently controlled by the image makers who package and market candidates for a passive electorate. The public debate appears dominated by various interest groups each clamoring for a piece of the shrinking economic and political pie. Civility and rational persuasion diminish as political discourse languishes in the murky depths once reserved for guests on television talk shows.

Clearly, I have offered a somewhat exaggerated picture of the plight of contemporary public life, but the description captures to some extent the sense we have of ourselves as alienated citizens. The question now arises: Is it possible to reconstruct the social conditions necessary for developing a more noble conception of citizenship, and can Christian churches play a role in that reconstruction? And further, how might our worship life contribute to the shaping of a new generation of Christian citizens? I will seek to answer those questions by developing a theological proposal regarding Christian worship and public responsibility.

If Christians are to contribute to the construction of a new public philosophy for American public life, then we must avoid the dual temptations that have perpetually faced every major American denomination, the temptations of liberal accommodation to the culture or sectarian separation from it. Christians need to reaffirm their distinctive Christian identity and *thereby* to make our contribution to American public life. Recovery of an authentic public voice and critical appropriation of religious tradition must go hand in hand. If we need role models in this regard, we should look to those Christian communities who have made the most salutary contributions to contemporary public affairs in recent decades—the historic black churches and post–Vatican II Roman Catholicism. These communities have maintained a set of ritual, symbolic, and theological practices that provide a coherent context for the lively, even feisty, disputes within their ranks. For all the religious disputes within these religious bodies, they remain identifiable traditions, communities engaged in serious debate and discussion about the proper interaction between faith and public life. The touchstone of a tradition is essential for a vibrant and authentic public voice.

The challenge to Christian churches in the United States today is to engage in a critical reappropriation of our historic traditions and thereby to develop an authentic public voice. We must return to the questions that so vexed our sixteenth- and seventeenth-century forebears: How might

120

churches function as "schools of virtue" while still emphasizing the primacy of God's justifying grace? How are we to understand the mission of the *koinonia tou Christou* and the *leitourgia* appropriate to such a community? How might our worship life serve to foster a sense of public responsibility among those who gather around the ministry of word and sacrament?

In order to launch our discussion about these important but complicated matters, I offer a series of theses.

1. *The church must rediscover the essential link between liturgy and catechesis, between worship and education.* In the early church, catechetical instruction was designed to prepare potential adherents for baptism by instructing them in the basic language and practices of the Christian community. Such education was designed to introduce catechumens not only to the beliefs but also to the form of life represented by Christianity. By the time these converts were asked to profess the faith of the church at the time of baptism, they also understood the contours of the new life they were expected to exemplify. In the baptismal act, God's Spirit bestowed a new identity, and the convert's confession "I believe" marked both the acceptance of that identity and the commitment to enter into the practices of the Christian form of life. Thus the triple washing of baptism and the threefold confession of the triune God signaled the beginning of a new life in which the convert, having been instructed in the rudiments of Christianity, now undertook that lifelong journey of faith seeking understanding.

Liturgy, of course, has been one of the most important teaching tools throughout the history of the church. Text, ritual action, liturgical movement, and visual images intertwine to manifest the living faith of the Christian church. For today's Christian, who participates in the life of the Christian community primarily through its Sunday morning worship, liturgy continues to be the primary setting in which the beliefs and practices of Christianity are communicated. We need to become much more self-conscious about the *teaching* function of liturgy. What are we communicating about the virtues and values of the Christian community in the words, actions, and images of our liturgy? How are we to interpret the meaning of ritual to those increasing numbers of Christians who enter our congregations without previous experience of their own tradition and with little catechetical instruction in any Christian context? What reforms must we introduce in the church's educational mission in order to assure that our worship is communicating and shaping those virtues most central to the Christian faith?

121

2. Churches can be models for public life of communities in which plural-istic citizenship is possible, communities that witness to the unity that can be affirmed in the midst of diversity. American public life is foundering in a sea of cultural, political, and moral pluralism. Although Americans have al-ways recognized the diversity within public life, we have only rarely ac-knowledged it as a positive attribute. The framers of the Constitution had a rather negative assessment of cultural pluralism. They identified cul-tural differences with "factions," that is, groups of citizens motivated by self-interest, seeking their own good over that of the commonweal. The governmental mechanism adopted in the Constitution is designed not to affirm diversity but to counterpose factions, thereby limiting the power of any one interest group to dominate public life. The irony of our society is that, although we celebrate our *cultural* pluralism, we view our *political* pluralism as problematic. Ethnic and cultural minorities are immediately categorized as "interest groups" when they enter the political realm. We desperately need new models for understanding the positive role of eth-nic, cultural, and religious pluralism in the political realm. There is some-thing deeply embedded in our American self-understanding that leads us to view our own diversity with suspicion. As a nation shaped by the values both of the Enlightenment and of Puritanism, we hold images of unity and universality in high esteem. Our founding documents asserted the equality of all human beings, even as we tolerated slavery and denied full rights of citizenship to women. Our Constitution guaranteed the "free exercise" of diverse religious beliefs, even as our public figures have encouraged the development of a Protestant "civil religion" that defined our common beliefs and values. We are genuinely perplexed about how we can affirm our pluralism without rending the fragile garment that constitutes our common public life.

"Now there are varieties of gifts, but the same Spirit; and there are varieties of service, but the same Lord; and there are varieties of working, but it is the same God who inspires them all in every one. To each is given the manifestation of the Spirit for the common good. . . . If one member suffers, all suffer together; if one member is honored, all rejoice together" (1 Cor. 12:4–7, 26). The Christian tradition does have a way of under-standing unity in diversity, one as yet unimagined in the public sphere. Although we have often raised this model as the standard for our own life, we have been reluctant (sometimes for good theological reasons) to offer this model as a solution for the problem of diversity within the public realm. Perhaps our reluctance to "go public" with this model is grounded in our recognition of how badly we in the church have exemplified the form of life St. Paul sets before us in this text. If the community to which God's Spirit has been promised is unable to manifest the unity born of diversity, then how can we expect the public realm to do so?

That line of reasoning, though it has a certain plausibility, is finally quite dangerous, for it can encourage the kind of complacency concerning public life that is the great temptation of our time. Instead of viewing the failures of our own corporate life as an occasion for repentance, we use those failures to justify our cynicism about corporate life in general. Instead of using our historical shortcomings as a goad to more vigorous action to reform our own communities, we allow them to serve as rationales for the futility of meaningful action in the public arena. But at a time when we lack appropriate models for "unity in diversity" within ecclesiastical and political life, we cannot afford the luxury of such "sideline cynicism." At a time when joint action for the common good is increasingly rare in both church and public life, we must dare to introduce our biblical and theological models into the public discussion, thereby witnessing to a way of life that affirms commonality in the midst of diversity.

3. *The most important public service the church can render to the world is to be a community of hope.* Dom Ildefons at Maria Laach and Dietrich Bonhoeffer at Finkenwalde were beacons of hope at a time of grave public danger in the history of Germany. By reminding their communities of the primacy of worship in the life of the church, they demonstrated that public responsibility is an essential aspect of Christian identity. These two figures traveled very different paths following 1935. Abbott Ildefons continued to sustain the spiritual and scholarly life of the Benedictine community at Maria Laach while firmly rejecting the Nazi cult of personality and nation. Dietrich Bonhoeffer took a more active path of resistance by joining the group of conspirators within the German *Abwehr* who ultimately sought to assassinate Adolf Hitler. But neither chose the path taken by so many other Christians in Germany—passive withdrawal from public life.

Our political challenge is clearly quite different from that faced by Christians in Nazi Germany, but there can be little question that we are in a period of crisis with regard to our public life. In such a situation, the primary public responsibility of Christians is "to give an account of the hope that is in us" (see 1 Peter 3:15), for hope is that virtue that is created within the Christian community but extends to the whole of the cosmos. The gospel proclaims that we find our life's justification solely in the crucified and risen Christ. As followers of the Crucified, we are called to a ministry in behalf of the poor, the outcasts, those on the margins of society. The way of the cross passes through urban ghettos and rural wastelands, through hospital rooms of the incurably ill and dying, through those deep corridors of despair within the hearts of those who are victims of abuse. Followers of the Crucified are called to identify with those who suffer. But as we walk the way of the cross, we are also called to proclaim the good news that the Crucified has risen, that suffering and despair are not the final judgment upon God's creation. Thus we are called to exemplify a "cruciform hope" within a world of despair and cynicism.

There can be little doubt that our public life is sorely in need of such chastened but genuine hope. We are assaulted by doomsayers who terrorize us with the specter of nuclear holocaust without providing either reasons for hope or genuine opportunities for action. They (and sometimes we are to be counted among them) proclaim a gospel of death without resurrection. At the same time, we are surrounded by multitudes who have turned their backs on the magnitude of the world's problems. Lacking the means or the power to effect significant change, they (and sometimes we are to be counted among them) turn inward and attend primarily to private and personal needs, not so much rejecting the public world as forgetting or ignoring it. Such forgetfulness transforms our hope for God's world into an introspective fixation upon our own selves. Our restless heart turns away from our neighbors in need and curves in on itself, and so we seek rest in the one place we will never find it.

A public theology firmly fixed on the gospel of the crucified and risen Christ can provide a witness true to our Christian heritage and yet relevant to the contemporary world. The ministry of word and sacrament must play an essential role in any genuine attempt to engage American public life, for it is through those means of the spirit that the theological virtues of faith, hope, and love are created and sustained. Those essential Christian virtues, which many have thought to be irrelevant to the realities of a secular public *ethos,* are the most precious gifts we can give to a world created by God but now groaning in travail, a creation that "will be set free from its bondage to decay and [will] obtain the glorious liberty of the children of God" (Rom. 8:21).

NOTES

1. Ildefons Herwegen, O.S.B., "The Nature of Religious Art," *Liturgical Arts* I (1931–32): 5–6, quoted in Ernest Benjamin Koenker, *The Liturgical Re-*

naissance in the Roman Catholic Church (Chicago: University of Chicago Press, 1954), p. 168.

2. Eberhard Bethge, *Dietrich Bonhoeffer* (New York: Harper & Row, 1977), 382.

3. Paul Lehmann, "Praying and Doing Justly," *Reformed Liturgy and Music* XVX:2 (Spring 1985): 79.

4. Stanley Hauerwas, *A Community of Character* (Notre Dame, Ind.: University of Notre Dame Press, 1981), 84.

5. Ibid., 74.

6. Martin Luther, *Lectures on Galations, 1535,* in *Luther's Works,* vol. 26 (St. Louis: Concordia Publishing House, 1963), 256.

7. Gerald Strauss, *Luther's House of Learning: Introduction of the Young in the German Reformation* (Baltimore: Johns Hopkins University Press, 1977), 300, as quoted in Gilbert Meilander, *The Theory and Practice of Virtue* (Notre Dame, Ind.: University of Notre Dame Press, 1984), 124. My discussion of Luther and Lutheranism is indebted to Meilander's insightful discussion.

8. William J. Wilson, *The Truly Disadvantaged: The Inner City, the Underclass, and Public Policy* (Chicago: University of Chicago Press, 1987).

7

PIETY, NARRATIVE,
AND CHRISTIAN IDENTITY

"Piety is the foundation of all virtues." That Ciceronian sentiment penned in the first century B.C.E. was a commonplace of ancient Greek and Roman philosophy. And yet such high praise of piety sounds foreign to the ears of persons reared in modern culture. Our attitude toward piety is more likely reflected in the irony of a venerable Spanish proverb: "Never leave your corn to dry before the door of a pious man!" We have learned to be wary of the profession and practice of piety, expecting it to be a pretense that hides some secret passion or arcane fanaticism. Indeed, one definition of the word *pious* offered by Webster's *Ninth New Collegiate Dictionary* is "marked by sham or hypocrisy."

It is odd that piety has come to connote that which is false and external, because the term was used in post-Reformation Christianity in an attempt to recover an authentic religion of the heart. Pietism, the movement spawned by Philipp Spener's *Pia Desideria,*[1] directed its sharpest criticism against the externality of doctrine and ritual. Piety, in contrast to such empty externals, was the true conviction of the heart that manifested itself in a disciplined moral life. Spener's reform had as its goal the instilling of "an earnest, inner godliness."[2] Unfortunately, the excesses and intolerance of the eighteenth and nineteenth century inheritors of pietism have shrouded the term *piety* in an unwholesome cloud. We are more likely to associate pietism with witchcraft trials than with the institution of Bible reading and family devotions in the home.

It may be that the term *piety* is no longer useful to describe the authentic spiritual life, but there are aspects of the term's seventeenth-century usage that deserve our careful attention. Spener's central teaching was that "it is by no means enough to have knowledge of the Christian faith, for Christianity consists rather of practice."[3] It is this key claim of pietism—that Christianity is essentially a practice—that I want to investigate in this chapter. If Christianity is a practice, then the formation of the Christian life becomes the central task of the Christian community. Everything within the community should be directed toward the edification of Christian identity. Theology as a crucial activity within the Christian community should also serve Christian practice. But how? Theology is commonly understood as a theoretical activity, and its relation to the practice of the Christian life is often unclear. I want to examine the relation between theology and Christian practice—or more precisely stated, between Christian theorizing and the formation of Christian identity. If we take seriously the priority of the practical within Christianity, how will this affect our conception of theology? How can theology serve the formation of Christian piety? How can a theoretical activity contribute to the practice of Christian faith and life? I will argue that the key to an appropriate understanding of theology and practice lies in a fuller appreciation of the *narrative shape* of the Christian life and of Christian theorizing. Narrative is the crucial category for reuniting the theoretical and practical in the Christian community.

THEOLOGY AND PRACTICE:
THE PROBLEM STATED

The suggestion that theology ought to serve Christian practice is hardly a novel proposal. Most contemporary theologians would undoubtedly accept such a general statement about theology's purpose. The more perplexing issue is how precisely theology and the Christian life should be related in order to enhance the formation of Christian identity. The problem is heightened by the fact that the activities of doing theology and living the Christian life appear so different or even opposed. Theology is a form of theorizing and bears the marks of all theoretical activity. It strives to be methodologically self-conscious, objective in evaluation, and abstracted from the confusing ebb and flow of everyday life. The activity of living the Christian life is less easily defined precisely because it is saturated with the ambiguity of the everyday. Christian practice is deeply influenced by custom and habit and is thus much less self-consciously methodic than is theology. Christian practice is a self-involving activity that does not prize objectivity and abstraction so highly. Although it is difficult to produce an exhaustive list of the characteristics that distinguish theoretical and practical activities, our commonsense assumption is that they differ in kind. And ever since the Greeks first distinguished *theoria* and *praxis,* we have associated objectivity and reflection with the former, and subjectivity and self-involvement with the latter.

The dilemma facing the theologian who seeks to unify theology and Christian practice is twofold. First, these two different and sometimes opposing activities must be brought together within a single framework. Second, they must be related in such a way that priority is granted to the practical. The difficulty is immediately obvious. How is one justified in granting priority to the activity characterized by custom, habit, and subjectivity? Surely priority ought to be given to theology with its goal of self-conscious objectivity. Only such a reflective activity would seem capable of giving normative guidance to practical action. Surely Christian life requires a norm abstracted from the ambiguity of the everyday by which to orient itself, a norm that must be discerned by theology. But if theology plays such an important role, how can it honestly be said that theology *serves* Christian practice or that the practical ought to have priority within the Christian community?

The complexity of this dilemma is most clearly revealed when we see how it shows itself concretely in the thought of a particular theologian. No theologian has had a greater influence on the development of modern theological method than Friedrich Schleiermacher. Most twentieth-century theologians have followed his methodological lead, and those who have resisted his influence have, nonetheless, been absorbed in criticizing him. Schleiermacher is especially important for our purposes, because he viewed himself as an heir of the pietist tradition. He held practical theology in the highest regard and restored the term *piety* to a place of honor in theological vocabulary. But Schleiermacher resisted the anti-intellectual tendencies of the pietist tradition and attempted to combine within a single method intellectual rigor and practical relevance.

I hope to show in the following section that Schleiermacher's noble attempt to combine theory and practice does not fully succeed. He fails because he adopts a view of theory that undermines his intention to give priority to the practical. Schleiermacher adopts the view that theoretical philosophical inquiry is *foundational* in character, that is, that it seeks to provide a universal justification for Christian faith. Consequently, philosophical theology, the most abstract and formal inquiry, becomes the key theological discipline. Subtly but decisively, theology is transformed from a practical study assisting the formation of Christian identity to a theoretical study seeking the universal form of religion. As long as theology continues to adopt a foundational view of theory, it will be unable to escape from the dilemma that plagues Schleiermacher's thought.

THEOLOGY AS FOUNDATION:
THE CASE OF SCHLEIERMACHER

"Theology is a positive science, whose parts join into a cohesive whole only through their common relation to a particular mode of faith, i.e., a particular way of being conscious of God."[4] With this definition, Schleiermacher combines theory and practice in an ingenious manner. Theology is a *science,* that is, a rational theoretical inquiry characterized by self-conscious reflection and objectivity. But theology, in contrast to other theoretical disciplines, is a *positive* science, that is, a rational study that is justified by the particular goal it serves. That goal of enhancing faith or God-consciousness provides the unity for the various methods operative within theology. Philosophical, historical, and practical theology may differ sharply with reference to method, but they are unified in that each seeks to facilitate greater consciousness of the believer's relation to God. Consequently, theology is practical in that its *goal* is to enhance the consciousness of God in the Christian life; theology is theoretical in that its *method* bears the marks of an objective scientific inquiry.

The distinction between goal and method would seem to be an apt solution to the relation of theory and practice. But Schleiermacher does not reckon sufficiently with the fact that scientific pursuits have goals that are independent of the particular subject matter they study. Insofar as a science *seeks* universal acceptance of its conclusions, such universality is a *goal* of scientific inquiry. And it is possible that the scientific goal of universality may conflict with a positive goal such as the edification of God-consciousness. If the scientific and positive goals do conflict, which is to be given precedence?

Schleiermacher does not provide an explicit answer to that question. His statements regarding the relation of theory and practice seem to presuppose the congruence of scientific and positive goals. When the two are in agreement, clearly primacy of place is to be granted to practice. Schleiermacher's well-known declaration "practical theology is the crown of theological study"[5] illustrates his commitment to the precedence of the practical. But a close look at his method in operation reveals that when theory and practice *conflict,* greater weight is to be given to theory. Logical priority in Schleiermacher's system belongs to the scientific investigation of philosophical theology. Theology as a science must seek the universal foundation of religious practice, for without such a foundation the practice of religion has no ultimate justification and no norm to guide its development. Though Schleiermacher fully intends to stress the priority of the positive practical goal, his conviction that theology is a scientific foundational enterprise finally thwarts his intention. In the end, the scientific and theoretical gains precedence over the positive and practical, and the crown passes from the head of practical theology to that of philosophical theology.

Philosophical theology must articulate the norm that is to guide the religious life by discerning the universal foundation of piety. The theologian surveys the diversity of voices manifest in worship, teaching, proclamation, and prayer, and seeks to discover the "common element" in these "diverse expressions of piety."[6] This "self-identical essence of piety" then serves as the basis and norm for all further development of religious practice. The philosophical theologian is charged with no less a task than discovering the universal essence of religion that will provide the ultimate foundation for belief and action. All concrete expressions of piety are to be evaluated with reference to this universal essence. Only those practices that accord with this philosophically discerned essence are authentically religious.

Philosophical theology thus becomes the crucial normative discipline within the church. It determines the essence of faith and the standard by which expressions of piety are to be evaluated. Without theology's foundational investigation, Christian practice remains blind and aimless. Because of the importance of its task, the reliability of theology's method becomes all the more important. If theology is to provide the foundation and norm for Christianity, then its method must be rigorously scientific. Inexorably, the scientific theoretical side of Schleiermacher's definition of theology begins to dominate the positive practical dimension. Ironically, the theoretical must predominate so that philosophical theology might render its service to the practical life. In order to serve as critic and reformer of Christian practice, scientific theory must be granted ultimate priority over the very practice it seeks to serve.

A scientific inquiry seeks conclusions that are formal, universal, and atemporal. Theology as science thus seeks an essence of religion that is beyond the particular influence of history and culture (formal), that is applicable to all persons in every time and circumstance (universal), in a realm beyond the ambiguous ebb and flow of temporality (atemporal). Schleiermacher's own attempt at philosophical theology in paragraph four of *The Christian Faith* exemplifies these three characteristics of scientific investigation. But precisely as scientific rigor is gained, theology's relevance for the practical Christian life appears to vanish.

In an argument that is both elegant and complex, Schleiermacher seeks to define the universal shape of piety: "The self-identical essence of piety is this: the consciousness of being absolutely dependent, or, which is the same thing, of being in relation with God."[7] Schleiermacher designates a universal human experience, the consciousness of being absolutely dependent, as the foundational experience of all religious piety. All human beings have a consciousness of their absolute dependence, that is, an experience of being dependent for their very existence upon a source outside themselves. This experience is not one of dependence upon any finite object in the world, such as our feeling of dependence upon parents. In every finite relation, we always exert some reciprocal influence upon the other person and thus are never absolutely dependent. But when we ponder the whole of our active and passive existence, we experience ourselves as ultimately dependent and in relation to an other. This other, however, is not a finite object or person, but the source of all possible persons and objects, God.

Through this ingenious movement of thought, Schleiermacher is able to identify a universal human experience as the experience of a relation with God. Every human being is in relation to God, and that essential God-consciousness can be discovered simply through a careful examination of our humanity. Though Schleiermacher begins by examining the diverse expressions of Christian piety, he concludes by discovering the *universal* form of human piety. Only such a universally applicable argument is sufficient to establish the foundation and norm for Christian practice.

It is important to realize that Schleiermacher claims to have discerned the *formal* shape of piety, that is, piety-as-such, prior to its combination with particular historical or cultural elements.[8] The essential shape of piety is always the same; it is the experience of absolute dependence. Every authentic religion will manifest piety's formal essence but will combine that essence with different particulars derived from different cultures and historical periods. Christianity shares with Islam and Judaism the God-consciousness implied in absolute dependence but differs from both in being a religion of redemption in which all things are related to Jesus of Nazareth.[9] Schleiermacher is clear, however, that those Christian particulars do not grant religious experience its universal foundational character. The essence of piety is foundational and normative for Christian thought and practice because it is purely formal.

The final key characteristic of universal God-consciousness is its *atemporality*. Schleiermacher characterizes the feeling of absolute dependence as an "immediate" experience, by which he means an experience that cannot be grasped under the usual categories of space and time.[10] The experience of God-consciousness has a purity that transcends common experiences of particular objects and particular times. God-consciousness is a pristine experience that defies easy categorization with cognitive concepts. Though language requires that we use categories to speak about it, the feeling of absolute dependence can never be reduced to the concepts we use to communicate it. God-consciousness takes us beyond the cognitive world of distinct subjects and objects, of particular times and places. But precisely because this experience is precognitive and atemporal, it is always momentary and fleeting, for as soon as we begin to reflect upon or speak about it, we lose its pristine quality.

Once this universal, formal, and atemporal essence has been discerned, it becomes the standard by which all Christian thought and practice is judged. All doctrines and proposals for action that purport to be Christian must be shown to be expressions of the feeling of absolute dependence. Schleiermacher argued, for example, that the doctrine of the Trinity should not be included within the corpus of Christian doctrine because it "is not an immediate utterance concerning the Christian self-consciousness."[11] As this example shows, the essence of piety as discerned through theology's theoretical inquiry is both the foundation and norm for all that transpires within the Christian community.

Schleiermacher's theological method is brilliantly conceived and has been justifiably influential. I do not intend to offer anything like a thorough criticism of his method but hope simply to point to some internal tensions and problems in his position. As I have shown, the most obvious difficulty in Schleiermacher's approach is that he has effectively reversed the relation between theory and practice. Clearly, theology has become the foundation discipline that analyzes, criticizes, and reforms Christian practice. Despite Schleiermacher's praise of the practical, the theoretical discipline of theology now wears the crown of preeminence. The relation between theology and practice is straightforward and undialectical. Theology is the judge and reformer of practice, and practice seems unable to challenge or reform the theoretical investigations of philosophical theology.

The key element in this reversal of theory and practice is Schleiermacher's conviction that the theologian must provide a universally valid foundation for the Christian community. Christian practice, moreover, must be given a theoretical justification that is independent of Christian particulars. The unspoken assumption is that a formal and abstract argument possesses greater validity than one that is particular and concrete. Schleiermacher's acceptance of that assumption leads him to embark on his search for the universal essence of piety. But that investigation yields an abstract account of a universal experience that seems barely relevant to the formation of Christian identity. Although Schleiermacher surely intended theology to guide Christian practice, his emphasis upon the formal and universal elements of piety runs counter to his own intention. Schleiermacher's view of theology as foundational threatens to turn the discipline into an abstract and arid study far removed from preaching, prayer, worship, and sacrament. Given the predominance of Schleiermacher's method among contemporary theologians, perhaps it is not surprising that we find ourselves in a perpetual quandary as to how theology ought to serve Christian faith and life.

THEOLOGY AND CHRISTIAN IDENTITY: FAITH SEEKING UNDERSTANDING

If theology is to be more closely integrated with the practice of the Christian life, then some common patterns of thought associated with the foundational view of theology need to be overcome. Theology ought not be contrasted to Christian ministry in a manner analogous to the contrast between theory and practice. Most theory/practice models conceive of the two activities as qualitatively distinct and grant reflective superiority to theory. When this distinction is applied to the Christian context, it distorts the essential unity shared by theology and the activities of Christian ministry. The theory/practice distinction elevates theory to a position of abstract reflection that obscures theology's practical intention. Theology, like all activities within the Christian community, has a single ultimate goal, namely, to sustain and nurture Christian identity. With reference to this goal, theology does not differ at all from the "practical" activities to which it is often contrasted, for example, preaching, teaching, and counseling. All these activities are carried out in order that believers might gain a deeper realization of the Christian identity bestowed upon them at baptism.

The theory/practice contrast seems appropriate only when theology is conceived in a foundational mode. A theology that seeks the universal essence of piety-as-such requires a kind of reflection foreign to preaching or counseling; such a theology is formal, abstract, and distanced from its

133

subject matter in order to achieve the objectivity appropriate to a scientific inquiry. But precisely when theology is conceived in this way, it becomes least able to aid in the formation of Christian identity. If theology is to be an identity-forming activity, then it must give up its pretensions to be a foundational inquiry seeking the universal form of religion.[12]

I am not denying that theology involves rational reflection or that some canons of objectivity are appropriate to it; I am simply trying to distance theology from a particular conception of theoretical reflection that has distorted theology's practical intention. Critical thinking can make an important contribution to the development of the Christian life, but that contribution is threatened when theology seeks to offer a universal theoretical justification for the Christian faith. When theology accepts this foundational role, it inevitably embarks upon a "transcendental" exploration; that is, it seeks the conditions of the possibility of Christian faith and action. Or put differently, when foundational theology comes upon the various expressions of Christian faith and life, it asks, "How is this possible?" and sets out to find a theoretical answer to its question. Even if it were possible to answer such a question, it is not at all obvious what relevance that answer would have for Christian identity. The questions of identity are "Who am I?" and "Who am I to become?" The transcendental answers of foundational theology hardly seem appropriate to those questions.[13]

The first step in developing a nonfoundational view of theology is to recognize the inescapable temporality of theological thinking. Foundational theology seeks an atemporal essence that is prior to all historical and cultural particulars. Although such views acknowledge the temporal and historical, they constantly seek the essence of faith in an unchanging realm beyond the transitory. To reject a foundational view of theology is to reject the search for atemporal essences. Theology is a thoroughly historical discipline that does its work in the midst of a community and its tradition. Such a theology acknowledges the diversity of expressions of Christian faith at any give time and throughout the development of the Christian tradition. It sees temporality as a crucial dimension of Christian faith as a living, developing social phenomenon. Nonfoundational theology accepts the culturally conditioned character of all human knowledge (including the knowledge of faith) as a sign that the transcendent God has become incarnate in human history and culture.

This renewed sense of temporality means that theology has a special relation to tradition. Tradition has been well defined as "an historically extended, socially embodied argument."[14] The Christian tradition is comprised of those voices of the past and present that debate the true nature of the Christian faith. Theology is not intended to be the arbiter among such voices, but the vehicle by which the arguments are voiced. Theologians carry on the conversation, not from a privileged position above tradition, but from within the polyphony of voices that constitute the Christian community. Augustine, Aquinas, Luther, Calvin, Schleiermacher, and Barth are among those voices, but so are the professor of theology at Luther Northwestern Seminary, the pastor of Grace Methodist Church, and the *Book of Common Prayer*. If the voice of the theologian is to be given greater weight in this conversation, it is not because he or she possesses a privileged office but simply because the voice is persuasive and worth hearing.

Theology must then presuppose tradition because tradition *is* the living, developing Christian community. In the same sense, theology presupposes faith and seeks through critical reflection to understand that faith more fully. Anselm's description of theology as "faith seeking understanding" continues to provide an apt account of the theologian's task.[15] The theologian speaks from within the community of believers and thus speaks from the commitment of faith. The theologian cannot adopt a standpoint of radical doubt or assume a hypothetical position of neutrality vis-à-vis the Christian faith. The theologian is seeking neither to justify nor disconfirm that complex phenomenon we call faith. The theologian strives simply to *understand* through critical reflection. The process of understanding may yield a radical criticism and reinterpretation of tradition, or it may result in a confirmation of many ancient formulas. The outcome of theological investigation cannot be predicted in advance precisely because the theologian operates within the temporal ebb and flow of history and community. But the goal of theology remains constant, namely, to understand more fully and more critically the Christian faith in order that the community might better exemplify the Christian identity to which it has been called.

It may appear that the view of theology I am recommending denies that theology is a normative discipline. The apparent advantage of the foundational position has been its claim to discern the unchanging essence of Christianity that then serves as the norm for Christian thought and action. If theology rejects foundationalism, then isn't the church left without a standard for evaluating the many voices within the tradition? That is an important question, and I cannot deal with it fully in this context.[16] But some comment is appropriate here.

The idea that we can discover the true essence of Christianity beyond the confusing din of cultural and historical voices is a tempting notion. But that is finally all it is—a temptation that we need to reject on philosophical and theological grounds. The post-Hegelian discussion in philosophy has raised serious questions about the possibility of discerning atemporal transcendental essences.[17] But even if the philosophical discussion were not decisive, the theological objections to foundationalism are. God's revelation has come to humanity through the history of the people of Israel and the life, death, and resurrection of Jesus of Nazareth. The heart of the Christian gospel is that God is known in human reality, that is, historical and cultural reality. God continues to be manifest through the reality of the created order—through the words of proclamation and the water, bread, and wine of sacraments. We must seek the heart of the gospel within human reality and not beyond it. God is revealed precisely where God has chosen to be hidden, within the "masks" of the creation.[18] Foundationalism is finally a sophisticated "theology of glory," which like all such theologies lures us into thinking that we can storm the heavens with our clever minds. We must rather be content to remain in history, to hear the voice of the gospel in proclamation and the biblical narrative, and to struggle to discern God's word for the church. The theologian does have a norm by which to work—the gospel as proclaimed in biblical narrative. The theologian has no privileged access to the gospel's essence but must hear it as all Christians do through written, spoken, and sung words. Informed by Christian practice, yet critically reflecting upon it, the theologian seeks to articulate the gospel so that through it God might mold our Christian identity. Informed by theology, yet not determined by it, the Christian community continues to be a tradition, an ongoing conversation about the nature of the Christian faith and life.

NARRATIVE, THEOLOGY, AND THE CHRISTIAN LIFE

Because nonfoundational theology emphasizes the temporality of human life, it is natural that "narrative" should emerge as its organizing category. If theology is to be a normative discipline, it cannot simply echo all it hears in the ebb and flow of history. The theologian must find a way of organizing the diverse witness of Christian history that respects its temporal character. Moreover, the mode of organization must ultimately serve the formation of Christian identity. Narrative becomes the key category, because its structure incorporates temporality in the element of *plot* and assists the formation of selves in the element of *character*.[19] As Stephen Crites has argued, "Narrative alone can contain the full temporality of experience in a unity of form."[20]

Narrative orders our experience through the development of plot. Our ability to "follow" a story depends upon the unique combination of succession and configuration within the plot.[21] Narratives move temporally; that is, events succeed one another in a temporal fashion. But mere succession does not enable us to follow the story. The events must be configured into a coherent whole that organizes the events without destroying their temporal succession. Successful narratives pull us along by creating expectations in the reader that the narrated events are moving toward some end or conclusion. To be sure, there is no straight-line progression of events to an expected conclusion. Good stories are filled with the unexpected, the sudden turn of plot, the coincidence—what Frank Kermode has called "peripeteia"[22]—as they move toward their endings. And yet when the conclusion has been reached, "it all fits"; that is, the configuration of events makes sense from the vantage point of the end. This quality of *ordered temporality* makes narrative a valuable tool for theology, for it provides a structure by which the theologian can interpret the diverse landscape of historical experience.

Narrative also provides the crucial category for the discernment of personal identity. Characterization is the second important element of narrative structure. Through the interweaving of setting and event, a narrative depicts the actions of characters. In a realistic narrative, characters are caught up in contingent events remarkably similar to those that mark our own lives. As we see the characters act and suffer within the framework of the plot, we come to know and understand them. Again, expectations are created in the reader as we anticipate the reaction of a character to an unexpected twist of plot. The term *character* is intentionally ambiguous, for it can describe both an actor in the narrative and certain traits of that actor that are "characteristically" human. In coming to know George Smiley in John Le Carré's novels, we discover something of the traits of patience, persistence, and loyalty. And in so doing, we learn more about ourselves, particularly whether we exemplify a similar character. Narratives thus present patterns of characteristic action that depict personal identity. The characteristic unity that allows us to speak of a person's identity in the midst of the diverse actions he or she performs is related to the configural unity of plot. Both plot and character are what Kermode has called "concordant-discordant wholes."[23] Despite the variety of action and event, finally a unity is discernible in both. And the unity of character is what we call personal identity.

This general discussion of plot and character shows how narrative analysis can be useful for a nonfoundational theology, but certain aspects of the theological use of narrative deserve more careful attention. Narrative gives the theologian a structure by which to interpret the temporality of human life in a way that contributes to the formation of Christian identity. But clearly, the theologian is in a different position from that of the novelist, who can simply create an imaginative configuration to depict a meaningful world with realistic characters. Clearly, there are countless potential narratives that can be told to make sense of our lives; the novelist is limited only by the constraints of his or her imaginative power and the readers' sense of plausibility. By contrast, the theologian seeks to offer a narrative interpretation that is not only coherent and elegant but peculiarly Christian as well. The theologian stands within a community and its tradition, and speaks not only personally but also for the community. Although the theologian's account will inevitably bear the marks of individuality, that account must finally accord with *the Christian narrative,* that is, that "discordant-concordant whole" that identifies the community as being distinctively Christian.

Certainly there are difficulties in speaking of *the* Christian narrative, as the historical critics will be quick to tell us, but the notion cannot be discarded simply because we recognize the diversity within Christian tradition. If Christianity is a community with a discernible identity, then there must be a story that depicts that identity. This story is certainly no seamless whole—but then no good narrative is! Although the Christian narrative cannot simply be equated with the biblical narrative, the grand narrative configuration of scripture is a key part of the overarching Christian story. The biblical texts depict the world within which Christian identity is to be sought. The accounts of God's action from creation through the election and history of Israel and culminating in the life, death, and resurrection of Jesus Christ provide the essential clues to the identity of the Christian community and of the God who brought it into being.

Of course, there are difficulties facing a theological interpretation of Scripture, particularly the danger of imposing a premature narrative unity on these complex texts. Despite such dangers, theologians must continue to seek the configural unity of the biblical witness, recognizing that good narratives are always discordant as well as concordant. The biblical narratives depict a world in which God and human beings interact. Often the actions of the human characters seem designed to flaunt the intention of the Creator. At other times, the plot takes such bizarre twists that no narrative unity seems apparent. Yet despite (and often because of) "peripeteia" in the development of plot and character, the narratives move toward a discernible conclusion. And as they do, the meaning of the overarching narrative begins to emerge. Occasionally, the narrator will offer an explicit interpretation of the action, but more often the meaning is carried through narrated action and dialogue.[24] Like an exceptionally rich novel, the biblical narrative provides the structures of plot, characterization, and setting that serve as the clues to the texts' meaning. But the act of interpretation is finally ours, and my argument in this chapter has been that such interpretation is the central theological task. Standing within the complex of Christian tradition, theologians need to risk interpretation of the biblical narrative in order to provide proposals for Christian belief and action.[25] The interpretations and proposals will differ, but that is to be expected within any living tradition. No single interpretation can ever claim to have discerned *the* Christian narrative, but all strive to be faithful expressions of it. The Christian narrative is a story that can never be fully told, for it is the story of a community that has not yet reached that *telos* for which God intended us. But we are not bereft of guidance, for in the biblical narrative, and particularly in the account of Christ's resurrection, we glimpse the end that awaits us. Until we reach that appointed end, we continue to tell the story and seek to exemplify the Christian identity depicted therein. The Christian narrative is thus the story *we tell* in part—haltingly and piecemeal in worship, preaching, and theology; and it is the story *we shall be told* in full, when the tale is complete, and we meet its Author face to face.

NOTES

1. Philipp Spener, *Pia Desideria,* trans. and ed. Theodore G. Tappert (Philadelphia: Fortress Press, 1964).

2. Ibid., 47.

3. Ibid., 95.

4. Friedrich Schleiermacher, *Brief Outline on the Study of Theology* (Richmond: John Knox Press, 1966), 19.

5. Ibid., 125.

6. Friedrich Schleiermacher, *The Christian Faith* (New York: Harper & Row, 1963), 12.

7. Ibid.

8. "The self in question here is the self that is not qualified by or determined by specific objects and energies located in its world. It is the self in its

original identity, in its being-in-such-and-such-a-way (*Sosein*). . . . Piety or religion is the name of the level of self-consciousness that is most decisive of all. . . . It is a consciousness of the self prior to all of its specific social and practical relations." Richard R. Niebuhr, *Schleiermacher on Christ and Religion* (New York: Scribner's, 1964), 183–184.

9. Schleiermacher, *The Christian Faith,* 52–60.

10. Schleiermacher's clearest statement on this matter is found in his second speech on "The Nature of Religion," in *On Religion: Speeches to Its Cultured Despisers* (New York: Harper & Row, 1958), esp. 45–54 and 87–101.

11. Schleiermacher, *The Christian Faith,* 738.

12. For an analysis and criticism of philosophical foundationalism in theology, see Ronald F. Thiemann, "Revelation and Imaginative Construction," *Journal of Religion* 61 (1981): 242–263, and N. Woltersdorff, *Reason Within the Bounds of Religion* (Grand Rapids: Eerdmans, 1976).

13. Cf. the discussion of Dietrich Bonhoeffer, *Christ the Center* (New York: Harper & Row, 1978), 27–37.

14. Alasdair MacIntyre, *After Virtue* (Notre Dame: University of Notre Dame Press, 1981), 207.

15. "Proslogion," in *St. Anselm: Basic Writings* (LaSalle, Ill.: Open Court, 1962), 1–34. Two modern restatements of Anselm's position deserve special mention. Karl Barth, *Anselm: Fides Quaerens Intellectum* (Richmond: John Knox Press, 1960). Barth develops the full methodological implications of Anselm's phrase. David Burrell, "Religious Belief and Rationality," in *Rationality and Religious Belief* (Notre Dame: University of Notre Dame Press, 1979). Burrell offers a formulation of Anselm's principle that is not subject to the usual criticisms of "fideism." Note especially the interesting notion of "pragmatic implication."

16. This issue receives much more thorough treatment in my book *Revelation and Theology: The Gospel as Narrated Promise* (Notre Dame: University of Notre Dame Press, 1985).

17. Of the many discussions of this issue, see especially Richard Rorty, *Philosophy and the Mirror of Nature* (Princeton: Princeton University Press, 1979).

18. "The whole creation is a . . . mask of God." Martin Luther, *Lectures on Galatians, 1535,* vol. 26 of *Luthers Works,* ed. Jaroslav Pelikan (St. Louis: Concordia, 1963), 95.

19. Cf. Stanley Hauerwas with David Burrell, "From System to Story: An Alternative Pattern for Rationality in Ethics," in *Truthfulness and Tragedy* (Notre Dame: Notre Dame University Press, 1977), 15–39.

20. Stephen Crites, "The Narrative Quality of Experience," *Journal of the American Academy of Religion* 39 (1971): 303.

21. See Paul Ricoeur's helpful discussion of this point in "The Narrative Function," in *Hermeneutics and the Human Sciences* (Cambridge: Cambridge University, 1981), 274–296.

22. Frank Kermode, *The Sense of an Ending* (London: Oxford University Press, 1967), 18.

23. "That the concordant tale should include irony and paradox and peripeteia, that making sense of what goes to make sense should be an activity that includes the acceptance of inexplicable patterns, mazes of contradiction, is a con-

dition of humanly satisfactory explanation." Ibid., 163. In his more recent book, *The Genesis of Secrecy* (Cambridge: Harvard University Press, 1979), Kermode stresses far more the dissonance and obscurity of narrative.

24. See Robert Alter, *The Art of Biblical Narrative* (New York: Basic Books, 1981).

25. I am not arguing that theological assertions should take narrative form. Theologians are not storytellers; rather, theologians need to use narrative analysis in order to interpret the stories that form the basis for theological assertions. The assertions themselves may take the discursive form usually associated with dogmatic theology.

8

THE FUTURE OF AN ILLUSION:
THE DISTINCTION
BETWEEN THEOLOGICAL
AND RELIGIOUS STUDIES

The thesis of this chapter is quite simple, namely, that the distinctions commonly drawn between theological and religious studies are conceptually confused. These distinctions result either from a faulty understanding of the concept "religion" or from the political effort to justify the study of religion within the context of the university. If we adopt a philosophically sound notion of religion, then the distinction between theological and religious studies begins to fade, and we recognize that these terms are rough descriptive equivalents for the same set of "field-encompassing fields."[1] Though the distinction is not conceptually justifiable, it has had an important political function in the struggle to establish the intellectual viability of the study of religion within American universities. That vital struggle continues, and thus it is important to ask whether this conceptually illusionary distinction has an enduring political function. The first section of this chapter will inquire into the conceptual issues surrounding the relation between theology and religious studies; the second section will offer a constructive proposal based upon a "cultural-linguistic" theory of religion.

It is important to indicate from the outset that I write from the point of view of one who works within the institutional context of a divinity school in a university that does not have a department of religious studies. Harvard Divinity School faculty members play a major role both in the preparation of students for Christian ministry and in the training of scholars in fields related to theological and religious studies. The Committee on the Study of Religion that oversees all doctoral work at the university (both the Ph.D. and the Th.D. degrees) is officially a committee of the Faculty of Arts and Sciences, but more than half of its membership is drawn from the Divinity School faculty. This institutional fluidity is both bane and blessing. It is bane in that the demands on the institutional resources of the Divinity School (both financial and faculty resources) are considerable, and the responsibility to provide adequate instruction in normative, historical, and comparative studies is daunting. It is blessing in that the committee draws from departments throughout the university (including, for example, from the philosophy of science), and thus the relevance of the study of religion for a broad range of disciplines is institutionally indicated. Moreover, this institutional fluidity provides a freer intellectual context within which to consider the relation between theological and religious studies. Our conceptual imaginations are not limited by rigid institutional or departmental constraints.

I mention my own institutional context not simply as a means of "truth in advertising" but primarily as a reminder that we cannot discuss the conceptual questions involved in relating theological and religious studies without attending very carefully to the institutional settings in which these programs operate. Too many essays in too many august journals have sought to address these questions through abstract philosophical definitions of religion that bear little or no relation to the actual communities of practice within which the study of religion takes place. Attention to communities of practice both within and without the university is essential to the philosophical task of conceptual clarification of the distinction between theological and religious studies.

THE RELATION BETWEEN THEOLOGY AND RELIGIOUS STUDIES

In his fine essay "Theology and Religious Studies: The Contest of the Faculties,"[2] Francis Schüssler Fiorenza has reviewed various misconstruals of the relation between these two field-encompassing fields. He has shown that any approach that seeks to contrast them by reference to categories like subjectivity/objectivity, epistemic privilege/methodological neutrality, or advocacy/disinterest fails to recognize the deep similarities between these humanistic forms of inquiry. Relying on the insights of contemporary hermeneutics, Fiorenza shows that all humanistic and social scientific studies are characterized by a "double hermeneutic" in which "pre-understanding" and "subject matter," knowledge and interest, are inevitably intertwined. Although I might choose a different philosophical vocabulary to express this point, I am in essential agreement with Fiorenza's argument and consequently see no reason to reproduce or amplify it. Any simple version of the faith/knowledge contrast cannot be invoked to distinguish theological and religious studies.

I want to examine in greater detail two significant proposals regarding the relation of theology and religious studies, those offered by Schubert Ogden and Edward Farley. Both scholars seek to define the similarities and differences of the two forms of inquiry without relying on any simplified contrast between faith and knowledge or its functional equivalents. Following my critical investigation of their positions, I will offer my own account of the relation of theological and religious studies, based upon a revised definition of religion and the forms of inquiry appropriate to the practices of religious communities.

Schubert Ogden

Schubert Ogden has throughout his distinguished career produced essays that define issues with such clarity that the subsequent discussion must begin with his arguments. His article "Theology and Religious Studies: Their Difference and the Difference It Makes" is just such an essay.[3] In it, Ogden counters those who seek to contrast theology and religious studies by asserting that theologians must appeal to "special criteria of truth" or must believe certain propositions to be true before they are rationally justified.[4] Proponents of such arguments use this line of reasoning both to distinguish theology from religious studies and to dismiss theology as a legitimate form of inquiry. "No form of reflection appealing to special criteria of truth can," these proponents argue, "be legitimate, since no assertion can possibly be established as true except by appealing to completely general criteria applicable to any other assertion of the same logical type" (103). Religious studies are thus both different from and superior to theology because scholars of religious studies accept only general criteria of meaning and truth as applicable to their fields.

In an ingenious response, Ogden defends theology against the charge of "special pleading" by showing the similarities between theology and religious studies on the question of the meaning and truth of religion. Neither field appeals to "special criteria of truth," because both are concerned with the most basic issues of human existence. Religion, Ogden argues, is a distinctive cultural response to the inevitable human need "to make sense somehow of our basic faith in the ultimate worth of life" (108). Religious studies is that field-encompassing field that is constituted by its fundamental attention to "this one reflective question as to the meaning and truth of religion, given our universal human question about the ultimate meaning of life" (108).

Christian theology does not have contrasting or contrary aims; it is rather a particular instance of religious studies' generic concern with the meaning and truth of religion. Christian theology, the appropriate form of reflection within the Christian religion, poses "the reflective question as to the meaning and truth of the Christian witness as an answer to our own question of faith as human beings" (118). Theology and religious studies are thus bound together by their common constitutive concern "to ask about the meaning and truth of religion" (114) and share as their common constitutive experience "our basic faith in the ultimate worth of life." Both fields appeal to general criteria of meaning and truth, because both seek to address a "universal question" (119) of human existence.

Are these deep similarities sufficient to obliterate all distinctions between theology and religious studies? No, answers Ogden, because the distinctive attention given by theology to the witness of the Christian faith "is not in the least among the necessary conditions of the possibility of the field of religious studies" (118). The constitutive question of Christian theology concerning the meaning and truth of the Christian faith is among the questions properly asked by religious studies but is not that field's constitutive question. Thus the distinction between theology and religious studies remains.

Ogden's conclusions in this article are clearly congenial to the thesis I am setting forth in this chapter, and yet I find the theory of religion he employs to support his position quite problematical. Ogden's overall argument rests upon an understanding of religion as a cultural and symbolic response to the "universal question" of human existence, that is, "our basic faith in the ultimate worth of life." The fundamental assumption of this argument is the conviction "that to be human at all is both to live by faith and to seek understanding" (106). Because religious studies and theology are forms of inquiry that arise out of the elementary human condition, they are governed by the universal rational criteria appropriate to this basic faith. They differ only in that theology is a particular instance of a more general mode of "faith seeking understanding."

Ogden does not seek, in this article, to justify his fundamental assumption regarding "basic faith," but he has defended this view at length in his classic article "The Reality of God."[5] In another context I have offered a critique of Ogden's position, arguing that his conception of "basic faith" cannot be sustained independent of the questionable foundational epistemology on which it rests.[6] Ogden's otherwise brilliant argument cannot escape the problems inherent in appeals to incorrigibility, self-evidence, and intuition as the basis for universal propositions. Moreover, his position is peculiarly incapable of engaging in serious dialogue with atheism, because the atheistic position is dismissed as a logical possibility *ab initio*. But there are further problems with Ogden's position that raise special issues for our consideration of the nature of religious studies. Most arguments regarding universal human experience can be shown to be arguments for particular experiences projected upon a general human screen.[7] The logical structure of the ostensibly common human experience is nothing other than the structure of a local, historically conditioned, and temporally specific experience for which universal status is inappropriately claimed. The diverse richness of human experience, and particularly the experience of those who have been marginalized and excluded, is thereby forced to conform to the exalted single paradigm.

Ogden's argument regarding the common features shared by theology and religious studies is sufficiently general to allow for considerable diversity in the various expressions of religious faith, but the fundamental structure of his argument concerning universal human faith seems clearly derived from Christianity. I would agree that the basic form of Christian experience is aptly described by the phrase "faith seeking understanding," but whether that notion applies equally to the vast variety of world-religious experiences can only be determined by a far more complicated argument than Ogden presents in his writings on this topic. Ogden's theory of religion has the status of a hypothesis until it is tested in relation to the many religious traditions that constitute the subject matter of religious studies.[8] Moreover, his assertion that religious studies is constituted by the "one reflective question of the meaning and truth of religion" requires further amplification before it can be accepted as a fully justified proposition. In particular, Ogden appears to propose that normative forms of inquiry have priority over historical and comparative methods in determining the constitutive questions of the field of religious studies. That assertion of priority itself requires further justification.

Schubert Ogden has successfully shown that Christian theology and related forms of normative inquiry within religious studies have no need to engage in "special pleading" in order to justify their status as rational forms of inquiry. He has not, however, shown that all forms of inquiry within religious studies do or should conform to the paradigm applicable to normative studies. His argument tends to reduce the diversity of methods and religious traditions appropriately studied within religious studies by the importation of a formal structure derived primarily from Christian theology. Thus, although I am in agreement with his intention to show the significant similarities between theology and religious studies, I find that the theory of religion he adopts undermines the essential claim he seeks to establish.

Edward Farley

No scholar has had a greater impact upon our thinking about theological education than has Edward Farley. His two major studies, *Theologia* and *The Fragility of Knowledge,* have defined the major issues facing theological institutions at the end of the twentieth century. Not surprisingly, his reflections on the relation between theology and religious studies are similarly clarifying.

Farley shares the conviction that theology and religious studies are often falsely contrasted with one another.[9] He recognizes the historical conditions that led to the creation of programs of religious studies and the need to distinguish these programs from the Christian divinity schools, seminaries, and religion departments from which they arose. And yet he acknowledges that the categories commonly used to draw those distinctions do not pass critical scrutiny. In response to this situation, Farley seeks not simply to provide conceptual clarification of the distinctions between the two field-encompassing fields but also to describe their common plight within the contemporary university.

Farley begins his discussion, as Ogden did, with a definition of religion as a personal and corporate response to a universal human experience. "The human being exists . . . in self-conscious anxiety about the meaning of its experience or destiny. Its most fundamental striving or desires . . . occur on an infinite horizon. When the human being responds to what it construes that infinite horizon to be . . . this anthropological structure generates religiousness or piety" (62).[10] Farley then identifies three "constitutive and pervasive" dimensions of religion: its concern with truth and reality (transcendent dimension); its presence in individual human experience (anthropological dimension); its expression in social and cultural forms (corporate/institutional dimension). Any adequate study of religion must address all three dimensions of human religiousness.

In defining theology, Farley does not limit its meaning to the specific context of Christianity but offers a definition that will apply to any tradition within which reflective-interpretive activity takes place: "Theology is the reflectively procured insight and understanding which encounter with a specific religious faith evokes" (64). This definition emphasizes the cultural and historical concreteness of religious traditions within

147

which theology as a form of reflective understanding takes place. Theology for Farley is primarily a mode of understanding and only secondarily a science or discipline. Further, although theological understanding takes place in the encounter with religious faith, the theologian need not be a "belief-ful" participant in any religious community. Thus Farley turns aside any notion that the theologian appeals to special criteria of truth available only within the community of faith.

Farley is particularly adept at relating theoretical discussions of theological education to actual institutional arrangements. He recognizes that the mere existence of a department of religious studies within the university creates institutional pressures to identify the unified principles of interpretation that justify this pedagogy and area of scholarship: "The existence of a program or department of religious studies raises the issue of whether there is a subject matter correlative to the department or faculty which would be distorted by distribution among various disciplines" (66). Religion, "an aspect of human experience which has specific historical and cultural expressions," provides, Farley argues, the essential unifying subject matter for the various methods and disciplines collected under the banner of religious studies. And because religion is a particularly complicated phenomenon, religious studies must employ a hermeneutic oriented toward its subject matter yet related to the "canons of universal scholarship" that function within the university.

That dual responsibility toward subject matter and scholarly canons creates a distinctive situation for the study of religion in the contemporary technocratic university, a peculiar plight that binds together religious and theological studies. The hermeneutical principles that ought to function within both fields stand in sharp contrast to the "data-oriented methodological commitments and disciplinary loyalties of the university" (70). And yet the pressures for acceptance within the university guilds have led practitioners of both fields to forgo their "hermeneutic principles of experientiality and reality" and to employ "data-oriented styles and methods" (71). Thus religious and theological studies have during the past two decades contributed to "the general poverty of interpretation so widespread in the university" (71).

Given the need to call the university back to its primary vocation of providing a critical interpretation of human experience in its rich variety, religious and theological studies can contribute to the aims of the university simply by being themselves, that is, fields of study interpreting one central aspect of human existence, religiousness. Religious studies should aim to explore specific historical religions and the structural similarities among them, and thereby "attempt to illumine religiousness itself," religion as an aspect of human existence. Theological studies, those forms of reflective-interpretive inquiry peculiar to historical traditions, contribute to the larger aims of religious studies by engaging "the claim of these faiths to truth and reality" and thereby uncovering "their experiential and human dimension (religiousness)" (75).

Because theological studies are related to specific religious traditions, they will have aims other than those associated with the university, particularly to provide critical reflection and reformation of the teachings and practices of that community of faith. Such "advocacy" is compatible with the university's hospitable attitude toward "strong convictions about the importance and relevance of the subject matter. . . . There appears to be nothing about the hermeneutic principles of theological study which compromises such advocacy" (78). Therefore, Farley concludes, "there is nothing intrinsic about either the hermeneutics of theological study or participation in a religious community" that necessarily violates "the general canons of the university" (78). Therefore, religious and theological studies ought to be welcomed among those voices that constitute the conversation of the contemporary university.

Farley's reflections on theology and religious studies offer an expansion and refinement of many of the points addressed by Ogden's earlier essay. Like Ogden, Farley grounds his argument in a theory of religion in which human religiousness and religious communities are understood as a response to a universal human experience. Both authors grant that human religiousness is manifest only in particular historical religions,[11] but both seek to identify the enduring aspects of human religiousness that pervade all religious traditions. The identification of that enduring element is crucial because it provides the basis for the claim that scholars of religious studies accept general or universal standards of scholarship and thereby contribute to the general aims of the university. Precisely because scholars of religious studies inquire after dimensions of universal human experience, they ought to be full partners in the conversations shaping the contemporary university. Insofar as scholars of theological studies also participate in such general or universal inquiry, they, too, deserve standing within the university.

Farley is particularly deft in balancing the particular and the universal in his definition of religion. Although the universal elements are especially important for the justification of religious studies within the university, Farley is always careful to attend to the historical particularity of religious traditions. Nonetheless, there is an unresolved tension in

Farley's position that deserves careful scrutiny: "There is no religion behind the religions. This means that there is neither an actuality nor an
ideality, that is an entity, an essence, a universal structure, an archetype,
to be the referent of the term 'religion' " (72). Human religiousness must
be discovered through the painstaking analysis of particular traditions
and the careful comparison of their structural similarities. Only then can
general notions of human religiousness be appropriately generated. Thus,
in answer to the important question of the unifying subject matter that
justifies the existence of departments of religious studies, Farley must give
a somewhat tentative answer: "In religious studies there is not a ready
subject but *the search for a subject*" (71, italics added).[12]

Farley exhibits a similar ambivalence when he seeks to justify the
presence of theological studies within the university. Theological studies
are appropriately found within the university only insofar as they contribute to the understanding of universal questions of human existence, that
is, only insofar as they are subspecies of religious studies. But given the
ambiguity concerning the subject matter of religious studies, the status of
theological studies is even more questionable. Farley struggles with this
issue in the final chapter of *The Fragility of Knowledge*.[13] He acknowledges
that his view of theology as "the wisdom and critical reflection attending
faith" (133) appears to contrast sharply with his case for theological
scholarship within the university. "The nonreligious aims of the university seem utterly incompatible with the aims of theological study" (179).
One senses the tension in this final chapter among Farley's various uses of
the word *faith*. He contrasts the "theological study that occurs within
and on behalf of a community of faith and the more distanced study of
that community's faith" (179) that occurs within the university. The
former is oriented toward "faith's actual reflective life"; the latter toward
"the understanding" of faith.

The reader is surprised by this (artificial?) contrast between faith's
reflective life and the understanding of faith, particularly in a position
that conceives of theology as a form of hermeneutical inquiry. Can the
difference between the subjective and objective genitive be as great as
Farley implies? Farley's solution to this internal tension is to suggest that
"in the university, the primary agenda of inquiry concerns religious faiths
as historical phenomena" (181). Theological studies in the university
should investigate the historical, social, and symbolic-linguistic "dimensions of religious faith as a historical reality" (181). By implication, concern with "faith's actual reflective life" seems to have no proper place
within the university.

Why is Farley so hard-pressed to find a place within the university for theology's sapiential and practical orientation? Why does he fail to emphasize the importance of theology's concern with reality and truth precisely for a university whose intellectual life is in a state of crisis? Why does a project that stresses the vitality of theological inquiry limit its relevance for the university to the concern with historical forms of interpretation?

I believe there are two primary reasons why Farley refuses to urge a more forceful positive role for theology within the university. First, Farley is not very hopeful about the intellectual atmosphere of the contemporary university and undoubtedly feels that theologians can pursue their agenda more easily by creating some distance between theological studies and the aims of the technocratic multiversity. If theologians are to play the primary role of critic, then they need sufficient independence from the university to maintain their critical perspective.[14]

Second, Farley's understanding of "faith" and "religiousness" makes it difficult for him to resolve the tension between the universal and particular aspects of religion. Specifically, Farley is unable to justify the university status of theology with reference to "faith's actual reflective life." I want to expand on this point and then move from my critique of Farley to my own constructive proposal about the relation of theological and religious studies.

A PROPOSAL

The theories of religion employed by both Ogden and Farley focus on the universal human experience to which religion, as an individual and corporate phenomenon, is the response. The methods of inquiry employed by practitioners of religious studies contribute to the scholarly aims of the university insofar as they investigate this universal experience with the "universal canons" of scholarship. Faith itself, however, remains beyond the reach of scholarly investigation, and even "faith's active reflective life" is not an appropriate object of study within the university.[15] Faith is the source of religion but cannot be the scholar's object of study, because it is by nature prereflective. This theory of religion provides a justification for theology within the university insofar as theology is a subspecies of religious studies. In Ogden's position, theological studies are fully justified because they represent a particular instance of the inquiry into the meaning and truth of religion that is the focal concern of religious studies. I have argued, however, that this justification is gained by a questionable projection of the logical shape of Christian theological inquiry on the whole of religious studies. In Farley's position, theological studies are justified within the university only insofar as they focus on religion as a historical phenomenon; consequently, the practical and sapiential concern of faith and theology remain in essential tension with the scholarly aims of the university. For both theologians, however, rational justification of religious and theological studies is related to an account of the *origin* of religion as a response to a universal human experience. Consequently, both theories of religion remain linked to the conceptual apparatus associated with foundational epistemologies in which *causal explanation* is the only adequate form of rational justification.[16]

I want to offer an alternative account of the relation between religious studies and theology, one that is congenial to many of the arguments Ogden and Farley set forward but is linked with a quite different theory of religion. This theory focuses on the aspect of religion almost completely ignored by both Ogden and Farley, the practices of communities of faith and the reflective activity appropriate to those practices. The chief logical difficulty that plagues the theories of religion employed by Ogden and Farley is the sharp contrast between the prereflective nonlinguistic basic faith and the various linguistic and structural expressions of that faith in historical religions. The rational justifiability of religious studies is gained by reference to the universality of basic faith, and yet the relation of the particular data of religions (their beliefs, rituals, and practices) to this universal religiousness remains unclear.

I will argue that an understanding of religions as "cultural-linguistic" or semiotic systems offers a more adequate conception of religious belief and behavior, and allows for clarification of the relation between theological and religious studies. If we bracket at the outset the question of whether religion is a response to some universal human experience and focus instead on the beliefs, rituals, and practices that constitute historical religions, we can avoid many of the pitfalls inherent in the theories of religion discussed above. In particular, we gain greater clarity on the way the faith and practices of religious communities can become the proper object of scholarly study within the university.

"Religions are . . . comprehensive interpretive schemes, usually embodied in myths or narratives and heavily ritualized, which structure human experience and understanding of self and world. . . . Stated more technically, a religion can be viewed as a kind of cultural and/or linguistic framework or medium that shapes the entirety of life and thought."[17] If we think of religion as a semiotic system—a complex web of interrelated signs, symbols, and actions—then the forms of interpretation appropriate to that system are aspects of what Clifford Geertz has called "thick description." Meaning is discerned not by tracing linguistic codes and symbolic actions to some postulated common source, but by discovering the patterns inherent in the "multiplicity of complex conceptual structures, many of [which] are superimposed upon or knotted into one another, which are at once strange, irregular, and inexplicit."[18] Interpretation, then, is not a matter of seeking general or universal explanations beyond the phenomena being described; rather, "such broader interpretations and abstract analyses" must be embedded within the practices being described and should be approached "from the direction of exceedingly extended acquaintances with extremely small matters."[19]

Practitioners of thick description do not eschew theorizing but seek to keep theoretical judgments closely matched to patterns of religious practice and belief discerned and described within the semiotic system. "Only short flights of ratiocination tend to be effective [in describing cultural systems]; longer ones tend to drift off into logical dreams, academic bemusements with formal symmetry. The whole point of a semiotic approach to culture is . . . to aid us in gaining access to the conceptual world in which our subjects live so that we can, in some extended sense of the term, converse with them."[20] The semiotic approach to religion thus softens the distinction between description and explanation so that the careful description of patterns of belief, practice, and ritual action becomes an essential part of the process of rational justification. The scholar's task is to "uncover the conceptual structures" embedded within religious traditions and to "construct a system of analysis" that will make the religious symbol system accessible to others.[21]

If we adopt a cultural-linguistic understanding of religion, then all forms of inquiry that uncover and clarify the patterns of behavior and conceptual structures embedded within religious traditions contribute to the task of religious studies. I am in agreement with Schubert Ogden's definition of religious studies as those forms of inquiry constituted by fundamental attention to the "reflective question as to the meaning and truth of religion."[22] Because theological studies are concerned with the normative inquiry into the meaning and truth of a particular historical tradition, they clearly contribute to the larger task characteristic of religious studies.[23]

Religious and theological studies are justifiably part of the fields comprised by the contemporary university because they employ methods of inquiry parallel to those of historians, anthropologists, sociologists,

philosophers, literary critics, and psychologists.[24] The intellectual justification of religious and theological scholarship need not appeal to the
problematic notion of a universal human experience to which religion is
the response. A cultural-linguistic approach to religion is clearly accept-
able within the contemporary university.

One strength of the cultural-linguistic view of religion is that it does
not separate faith and its practices from the proper scholarly investigation
of religious traditions. The scholar of religion is like the ethnologist in-
vestigating a culture or a literary critic interpreting a text. The scholar
must seek to gain sufficient familiarity with the patterns of belief and
action within the religion so as to provide a description of the rich texture
of that tradition. In providing a "thick description" of religion under an
analytic scheme that identifies and depicts the tradition's conceptual
structure, the scholar of religion has contributed to the elucidation of
that tradition's *faith*. Religious faith, in a cultural-linguistic scheme, is no
"ghost in the machine"; it is not a prelinguistic or prereflective experience, but a set of convictions displayed "in, with, and under" a community's beliefs and practices. Thus the description and analysis of the
linguistic codes and symbolic actions of a tradition is a description and
analysis of the faith of that religious community. There is no conflict
between "faith's historical reality" and "faith's reflective life" in a cultural-linguistic model.

The various forms of inquiry within religious studies will have different aims, and it is with reference to such aims that Christian theology
finds its distinctive rationale. Theological inquiry has the particular aim
of seeking a critical reconstruction of the identity of the community
within which it operates.[25] This critical and reconstructive task is not
qualitatively different from the humanistic and social-scientific disciplines
that have practical aims; nor does it differ significantly from the aims of
scholarship appropriate within professional schools of medicine, law, and
education. The aim of critical reconstruction of communal identity does,
however, distinguish theology from the other disciplines within religious
studies; but for the purposes of my argument, I want to stress the relation
of this task to the descriptive and analytical tasks I have already identified.
Formation of religious identity is a further extension of the activity characteristic of the cultural-linguistic investigation of religion. The rich description of religious rituals and beliefs and the depiction of the patterns
characteristic of a religion are essential to the actual practice of the religion. An effective "thick description" of a religious tradition opens up a
vast religious world inhabited by fascinating characters, beguiling myths,

and enticing rituals. For some, entrance into this world is a momentary "dwelling within" a fictive universe at once entrancing and daunting, but the encounter does not significantly transform their identities. For others, this world becomes an inhabitable land, one in which the beliefs and practices begin to shape their character and transform their identities.[26] The transformative power of texts and traditions is not unique to the study of religion; scholars who teach in many fields (one thinks particularly of anthropology, philosophy, and literary studies) experience it regularly in themselves and their students. The crucial difference lies in the fact that many religious traditions have extant communities of practice within which the fictive possibilities of a text can become realized. Indeed, theologians have a special responsibility for interpreting their traditions with a view toward the critical reconstruction of communal religious identity. But this responsibility is simply an extension of the task of "thick description." To the already identified tasks of description and analysis, the theologian adds the goal of critical reconstruction.[27]

If time and intellectual resources permitted, I would want to argue that the goal of critical reconstruction of communal identity is the proper aim of all fields within religious studies that are related to living communities of faith. For both conceptual and sociological reasons, however, I must limit that claim to Christian theological studies. Insofar as the study of other religious traditions includes interpretive and reconstructive activity formally analogous to Christian theology, I expect that such an argument could be made with reference to those traditions as well. My training as a Christian theologian and my limited knowledge of other religious traditions leads me to be circumspect in developing that argument myself. Sociologically, the development of theological and religious studies has been intimately linked (both positively and negatively) to Christianity. Thus the discussion of the relation between theology and religious studies has focused primarily on the status of Christian studies within the university. With the decline in the cultural hegemony of Protestant Christianity in the United States, however, and with the increasing prominence of other religious traditions within our own culture, the sociological conditions for a broadening relation of religious studies to living communities of faith may be emerging. The current discussion within the Association of Theological Schools regarding membership criteria and accreditation for "ministerial" programs in traditions other than Christianity and Judaism is undoubtedly the beginning of a conversation that may have significant implications for the long-term relationship between theology and religious studies.

CONCLUSIONS

I would like to conclude these reflections by offering some musings about future institutional arrangements for the study of religion within the university.[28] I have tried to show in this chapter that the arguments that seek to distinguish theological and religious studies are either conceptually suspect or depend upon a faulty theory of religion. If we adopt a cultural-linguistic conception of religion, we discover that theological inquiry is a natural component of the thick description of religious traditions. Theological studies thus quite naturally belong within the university and can be equally well housed within departments of religious studies or within divinity schools. Given the importance of theology's reconstructive aim, however, the university-related divinity school may have a particularly vital role to play in this period of transition within American culture. Precisely because it is a hybrid institution, related both to the aims of the university and to the aims of communities of faith, the university divinity school can be a fertile experimental ground for the future relation between theological and religious studies. As a theological institution within the university, it can witness to the reconstructive aim inherent within all religious studies. As a historically Christian institution within a pluralistic university, it can be an important proving ground for the development of programs that reflect the reality of religious pluralism within theological curricula. The university divinity school can offer an environment in which scholars of theological and religious studies discover and emphasize their common plight and common destiny, and work together to make the contemporary university a more hospitable place for the study of religion.

NOTES

1. This phrase is used by Stephen Toulmin in *The Uses of Argument* (Cambridge: Cambridge University Press, 1969) to describe those fields of study that employ methodological approaches associated with a variety of disciplines.

2. Francis Schüssler Fiorenza, "Theology and Religious Studies: The Contest of the Faculties" (unpublished manuscript). I will cite this essay from the typescript made available by the author.

3. Schubert Ogden, "Theology and Religious Studies: Their Difference and the Difference It makes," in *On Theology* (San Francisco: Harper & Row, 1986), 102–120.

4. The language concerning rational justification is my own. Ogden states the issue as follows: "The theologian as such has to be a believer already committed to the truth of the assertions that theological reflection seeks to establish." Ibid., 103.

5. Schubert Ogden, "The Reality of God," in *The Reality of God* (New York: Harper & Row, 1966), 1–70.

6. Ronald F. Thiemann, *Revelation and Theology: The Gospel as Narrated Promise* (Notre Dame: University of Notre Dame Press, 1985), 5–6.

7. I have argued this point in some detail with regard to Lessing's view of religion in "Gotthold Ephraim Lessing: An Enlightened View of Judaism," *Journal of Ecumenical Studies,* 18, no. 3 (Summer 1981): 401–422. Not only is Lessing's position conceptually problematic, but it also has significant (though unintended) anti-Judaic consequences.

8. George Lindbeck has made a similar criticism of Bernard Lonergan's theory of religion: "Because this core experience is said to be common to a wide diversity of religions, it is difficult or impossible to specify its distinctive features, and yet unless this is done, the assertion of commonality becomes logically and empirically vacuous." *The Nature of Doctrine* (Philadelphia: Westminster Press, 1984), 32.

9. My analysis will be based primarily on Farley's article "The Place of Theology in the Study of Religion," *Religious Studies and Theology* 5 (1985): 9–29. In revised form, it appears as Chapter 4 of *The Fragility of Knowledge* (Philadelphia: Fortress Press, 1988), 56–82.

10. Farley's definition of religion focuses on the *origin* of religious piety or sentiments, thus following the most common paradigm in modern discussions of religion. In its fascination with origins, however, this view of religion participates in the questionable intellectual strategies of epistemological foundationalism. Cf. Thiemann, *Revelation and Theology,* 1–46.

11. "Religion never exists in general, any more than any other form of culture does, but always only as *a* religion, which has its origin and principle in some particular occasion of insight." Ogden, "Theology and Religious Studies," 110. "There is no religion behind the religions. This means that there is neither an actuality nor an ideality that is an entity, an essence, a universal structure, an archetype, to be the referent of the term 'religion.'" Farley, *The Fragility of Knowledge,* 72. Farley's more careful treatment of this issue makes his position less vulnerable to the foundationalist critique I offered of Ogden's position. It is also important to remember that Farley's essay was written seven years later than Ogden's and during the time when the philosophical critique of epistemological foundationalism was in full swing.

12. If this statement is true, then it is not at all clear that "there is a subject matter correlative to the department or faculty [of religious studies] which would be distorted by distribution among various disciplines." Farley, *The Fragility of Knowledge,* 66.

13. Farley, *The Fragility of Knowledge,* 171–191.

14. I think that Farley overstates his case with regard to the plight of the contemporary university and also gives insufficient attention to those forces in fields outside of theology and religious studies (one thinks of literary criticism, political philosophy, and anthropology) that are equally critical of the research aims of the technocratic fields and disciplines.

15. This is certainly the case for Farley. By contrast, Ogden would clearly allow investigation of faith's reflective life within the university.

16. I have discussed the problems inherent in the confusion between causal explanation and rational justification in *Revelation and Theology*, 43–46.

17. Lindbeck, *The Nature of Doctrine*, 32–33.

18. Clifford Geertz, "Thick Description: Toward an Interpretive Theory of Culture, in *The Interpretation of Cultures* (New York: Basic Books, 1973), 10.

19. Ibid., 21.

20. Ibid., 24.

21. Geertz rightly warns against making coherence "the major test of validity for a cultural description. Cultural systems must have a minimal degree of coherence, else we would not call them systems; and, by observation they normally have a great deal more. But there is nothing so coherent as a paranoid's delusion or a swindler's story. The force of our interpretations cannot rest, as they are now so often made to do, on the tightness with which they hold together, or the assurance with which they are argued. Nothing has done more, I think, to discredit cultural analysis than the construction of impeccable depictions of formal order in whose actual existence nobody can quite believe." Ibid., 18.

22. Though I would not add, as he does, "given our universal human question about the ultimate meaning of life."

23. For an account of theological method that is congenial to this view of religious inquiry, see Chapter 4 of my *Revelation and Theology*, "Toward a Nonfoundational Theology," 71–91.

24. George Lindbeck describes the growing influence of the cultural-linguistic approach in various disciplines in *The Nature of Doctrine*, 19–29.

25. This point has been made in a number of ways by different theologians. David Kelsey speaks of the role of scripture in the Christian community as one "shap[ing] persons' identities so decisively as to transform them." See David Kelsey, *The Uses of Scripture in Recent Theology* (Philadelphia: Fortress Press, 1975), 91. Francis Schüssler Fiorenza signals theology's distinctive task of "engaging in the reconstruction of its identity in the face of contemporary practice." See "Theology and Religious Studies: The Contest of the Faculties," 22. I have developed the important role that theology plays in the reconstruction of Christian identity in two essays. In "Piety, Narrative, and Christian Identity," *Word & World* 3, no. 2 (Spring 1983), I argue that "the goal of theology" is "to understand more fully and more critically the Christian faith in order that the community might better exemplify the Christian identity to which it has been called." In "The Scholarly Vocation: Its Future Challenges and Threats," *Theological Education* 24, no. 1 (Autumn 1987): 97, I define theology as "the critical reflection on religious practices." One essential aspect of the theological task is "the formation of religious identity and character."

26. It is useful in this regard to reflect on the ambiguity inherent in the word *identity*. On the one hand, the word specifies an act of description (e.g., the identification of the ritual practices of the Nuer or the plot line of Jane Austin's *Emma*); on the other hand, the word specifies a personal act of commitment and character formation (e.g., identification with the plight of the Nicaraguan refugees or the women followers of Jesus in the Gospel stories).

27. For one example of how critical reconstruction grows out of descrip-

tion and analysis in the Christian tradition, see my *Revelation and Theology*, 71–156.

28. I am not convinced by the contrast drawn by both Ogden (106) and Farley (66) between studies of religion and religious studies. Studies that are relevant to the thick description of religious traditions are found in many fields and disciplines throughout the university, and we limit the range of resources we need for our common task by drawing too sharp a distinction between studies of religion and religious studies. With regard to this issue, the emergence of *departments* of religious studies may represent an unhappy constraint on the study of religion within the university. If the study of religion is institutionally limited to a department (with all the funding and staffing restrictions thereby implied), then the scope of programs in religion will be severely constrained. Ideally, religious studies should have the status of *area studies* in which the resources dealing with religion in various university departments are brought together. But until the day dawns when the university encourages the study of religion within manifold disciplines, the department of religious studies remains an essential holding operation.

9

TOWARD A CRITICAL
THEOLOGICAL EDUCATION

Before I entered the field of theological education, I spent my entire teaching career at a liberal arts college. As I made my way through the first months of my deanship at Harvard, I came to recognize that the challenges I faced as a teacher, scholar, and administrator in the interdisciplinary context of the liberal arts are not all that different from those I face as head of an interdenominational university-related divinity school.

For a decade, I have sought to reflect on the peculiar challenge of teaching Christian theology within the humanities division of a secular educational institution. The liberal arts setting of the small college encourages a great deal of interdisciplinary conversation; one's closest colleagues are often in departments other than one's own, and so it becomes necessary to familiarize oneself with diverse but related disciplines. My own teaching and research have been deeply influenced and immeasurably strengthened by exchanges with philosophers, social theorists, historians, and anthropologists on the Haverford College faculty.

One of the lessons I have learned from those conversations is that such exchange requires a combination of openness and self-confidence on the part of both conversation partners. Each must have a clear sense of what he or she can contribute to the conversation, even as together they seek to gain new insights from one another. Interdisciplinary cooperation can quickly come to an end if the conversation becomes too one-sided, if one partner tends to dominate to the detriment of the other. The goal of this kind of cooperation is not to create some new discipline or interdisciplinary department, but to create a new community of discourse, a group of people who identify a number of issues or questions they face in common and who seek to engage in mutually beneficial investigation of those problems.

I call attention to these reflections on my previous educational experience, because I believe that participants in theological education can learn a great deal from the conversational paradigm that I have briefly described. We have entered a period of great excitement in theological education; many of the old scholarly verities have been challenged, and many of the standard forms of education have been discarded. During the past decade, we have witnessed the rapid rise of liberation and feminist theologies and the dramatic shift in the gender and age distribution of our student bodies. We have all come to recognize the importance of cultural, ethical, and religious pluralism and have sought to diversify our curricula while still struggling to find some principle of coherence to hold it all together. Some mornings we awaken enormously stimulated by the bracing excitement of this ferment; on other mornings, we pull the covers over our heads fervently hoping to avoid the cacophonous confrontation of that collection of competing interests we call our faculties.

DEFINING STANDARDS FOR EXCELLENCE

There can be little question that we are still in a time of shifting foundations and unsettled priorities. It would surely be a mistake to define prematurely a curricular center or principle of coherence. At the same time, we must raise the question of whether we can begin to identify the criteria and standards for excellence in scholarship within theological education. If we cannot begin to define those criteria, then we face the unpleasant alternatives of borrowing standards from other fields that may not be appropriate for theological scholarship or abdicating our responsibility for developing and setting standards for the subfields within theology. In either case, the integrity of theological scholarship is threatened.

We face a number of difficulties in seeking to address the question of the future of theological scholarship. The extraordinary diversity of our disciplines, which range from philological and archaeological studies to practical courses in communication and parish administration, suggests a vast and impossible array of standards. What could possibly unite these various disciplines? What criteria of excellence might they hold in common? What principles of coherence bind together a seminary or divinity school community? In particular, do the traditional theoretical disciplines—historical, philosophical, and hermeneutical studies—have

161

anything in common with the practical disciplines: arts of communication, counseling, and pastoral care? Indeed, are practitioners within these
latter areas properly defined as scholars, and are they engaged in the kind
of research activity we should describe as scholarship?

There are additional difficulties. Liberation theology has brought
political categories to prominence within theology. How are we to distinguish appropriate political analysis from an inappropriate *politicizing* of
theological scholarship? And finally, how do we discern and encourage an
appropriate future for scholarship in theology? As we build our faculties
for the twenty-first century, what kind of research should we encourage?
Are there new fields we should seek to develop, and should other fields be
allowed to die unlamented deaths?

RAISING THE DIFFICULT QUESTIONS

The enormous range and complexity of these problems might lead
us to despair of seeking solutions. Perhaps we should simply allow ourselves to muddle through, trusting that a process of natural selection will
determine the future of theological scholarship. To some extent that will
undoubtedly happen; good arguments and solid research will inevitably
survive the trends and fads of any contemporary moment. But a laissez
faire attitude toward these matters could leave us unable to respond to
the peculiar demands of contemporary intellectual and religious life. I am
convinced that we need to raise the difficult questions about the future of
theological inquiry, even if we do not see the precise ways in which we
will answer them. In the midst of the stimulating diversity of theological
education, we need to seek those elements that provide a sense of coherence in our common intellectual task. We need to define more clearly
what we mean by the word *theology*.

In particular, we need to address three closely related issues. First, in
what sense is seminary and divinity school education genuinely theological? Second, how is theology, rightly understood, a critical discipline, and
how might it serve both to unite the various aspects of our curricula and
enable us to be better conversation partners with those outside the theological world? And third, what is the relation between the theoretical and
practical aspects of our educational programs, and how can those aspects
be integrated into a critical theological education?

Until we reach some agreement on the nature of theology as a critical discipline, we clearly will not be able to discern the standards for
excellence in theological scholarship or to project a future for our com-

mon endeavor. Of more importance, until we gain some clarity about what theology is and why it is important, we will be unable to make a contribution to the crucial intellectual, political, and social problems facing our world today. If theology remains in its current state of disarray, it will continue to play a marginal role in American intellectual life, and theologians will have little influence on debates within either religious or political communities. If we want to engage in a critical conversation with those outside of the theological disciplines, then we must have a clearer sense of what we can contribute to that conversation precisely as Christian theologians. If we do not have a sense of the nature and significance of our own theological discourse, then we can hardly expect others to find what we say interesting or important.

THE HISTORY
OF THEOLOGICAL EDUCATION

I want to offer a conception of theology as a normative, critical, and public discipline. But before I develop my proposal for what I hope is a broader and more inclusive understanding of theology, I need to review in brief compass some of the history of theological education that has brought us to our current situation. I will refer liberally to Harvard's place within this history. I do that not because of any particular pride of place but simply because it is the history I have come to know the best.

In 1808, immediately following the Unitarian Controversy sparked by the election of Henry Ware as Hollis Professor of Divinity at Harvard, a separate theological faculty was established by orthodox congregationalists at Andover. The founding of Andover Theological Seminary marked the beginning of professional theological education in the United States. Harvard liberals, unwilling to concede victory to the more conservative Calvinists, began planning for the establishment of their own independent theological faculty. On July 17, 1816, the Society for the Promotion of Theological Education in Harvard University was established, thus beginning a process that led to the founding of a "faculty of theology," or Theological Seminary, at the university.

It is important to note the place of theological studies within the broader university at this time. If we use Harvard College as our example, it is clear that by the beginning of the nineteenth century, undergraduate education had moved quite far from the founders' original concern to provide a literate ministry to the churches. By the time of the founding of the Harvard Divinity School, Harvard men were educated in a broad curriculum oriented more toward liberal education than ministerial studies. Prior to the nineteenth century, of course, theological training was an integral part of university education. At Harvard, every student was instructed in classical languages, rhetoric and grammar, and natural philosophy, studies that prepared the student for a better grasp of God's revelation within scripture and the natural world. During the eighteenth century, Harvard's president was responsible for the final year of instruction in divinity, the capstone of a student's university education. By the turn of the century, however, theological instruction was limited to the courses offered by the Hollis Professor, and there were no advanced courses in theology for those preparing to enter the ministry. As natural philosophy gave way to the natural sciences, a new understanding of critical reason emerged within European and American universities, one that did not so easily support the faith and piety that undergirded studies in divinity. By 1816 it was not self-evident that theological training ought to be a fundamental aspect of a general university education.

The founding of the first professional theological schools thus marked an important shift in the rationale for theological education. Training in divinity was no longer essential to those studies constituting a liberal education, but had become the course of studies appropriate for those entering into a specific profession, the Christian ministry. Thus, precisely as the ministry gained professional status, the *intellectual* justification for theological education became blurred.

The uncertain place of theological education within the general university context was highlighted during the so-called conflict of the faculties that occurred in Germany in the later eighteenth century. With the founding of the modern universities at Halle and Göttingen, a new understanding of rationality (*Wissenschaft*) came to dominate German intellectual life. A rational, or scientific, discipline is defined as one characterized by autonomous, critical, historical inquiry. Rational inquiry accepts no authority other than that of autonomous reason and seeks the truth unhindered by dogma, tradition, or institutional hierarchy. Given that definition of *Wissenschaft,* it is surely not self-evident that theology has a place within the modern scientific university. Indeed, in the eighteenth-century debate, Johann Fichte argued that because theology was founded on revelation and faith, it ought to be denied academic standing in the university.

Other eminent scholars, however, came to the defense of theology and thereby secured its place in the modern university, but the arguments they offered in support of theological education served further to undermine the intellectual standing of theology. Immanuel Kant and Friedrich

Schleiermacher both offered pragmatic arguments in support of theology within the university. Kant argued that the theological faculty, like the faculties of medicine and law, offered essential service to the state by training clergy for leadership roles in the churches. Schleiermacher developed a more sophisticated argument, but one that depended on the cultural assumption that religious piety is an indispensable social practice. Theology provides the skills and knowledge correlative to the indispensable practice of piety in the same way that medicine and law undergird the indispensable practices associated with health and the social order. The three faculties train persons for positions of leadership in the institutions designed to promote and develop these necessary societal practices.

These arguments, which are designed to secure both the professional status of the Christian ministry and the essential role of theology within the university, do not travel well across the Atlantic, because they depend upon assumptions that are difficult to sustain in a pluralistic, liberal democracy. Kant's argument presupposes a state established and supported religion, a constitutional impossibility within the American democracy. Schleiermacher's position rests upon a conviction that religion, and particularly Christianity, is an indispensable social practice. Although that contention might still receive some support in our contemporary culture, it is a controversial and debatable assertion. And surely the one place where it is least likely to gain widespread support is within the intellectual culture of the American university. The tendency of American theological educators to borrow our intellectual rationale from Europe has impeded our ability to develop a distinctively North American approach to theology, and it has aided and abetted the intellectual marginalization of theology within American society.

In the midst of this marginalization of theology, a strategy did emerge for relating at least some of the disciplines within seminaries and divinity schools to broader developments in American intellectual life. The commitment to critical historical studies has provided a powerful justification for the inclusion of biblical studies, and more recently the history of religions, within the university. But the focus on critical studies has not provided a justification for other aspects of the curriculum, particularly systematic and pastoral theology. Indeed, critical inquiry within the theological curriculum has often been very narrowly defined, eliminating from its purview any hint of normative investigation or evaluation.

The strong philological and archaeological orientation of the biblical departments at Harvard is just one example of the sharp distinction between critical-historical studies and normative theological studies in

American theological education. It is arguable that this strategy allowed divinity schools to maintain good university relations during the period of positivism that dominated university life from the 1930s to the 1960s. But it is also arguable that this strategy has become outmoded and irrelevant in a very different social and intellectual environment within the contemporary university. The distinction between objective (or "hard") historical studies and subjective (or "soft") normative studies is a false distinction, one that has contributed to the current fragmentation within theological education.

WHERE WE ARE TODAY

We find ourselves, then, in the following ironic situation. On the one hand, separate programs of professional ministerial studies have been justified by an argument for the social necessity of Christian piety, an argument that has, first, diminished in persuasiveness in the 170 years since the founding of the first independent divinity schools, and second, has separated those programs from the mainstream of American intellectual life. On the other hand, a program of critical religious studies within the university has been justified by an argument from objectivity that eliminates theology from the core of critical studies. The irony of this dual argument is that the justification for ministerial studies fails to establish the intellectual status of the curriculum, and the argument for critical studies, although providing a justification for some disciplines within the university, appears wholly disconnected from the preparation for ministry.

As questions of faith, commitment, and value became increasingly alien to "objective" critical studies, the internal connection between theology and practice was severed. The so-called theoretical fields have developed into discrete disciplines with their own professional societies and journals, and the technical, specialized research emerging from these disciplines has little or no relevance for ministry in religious communities. At the same time, practical studies, unleashed from their theoretical counterparts, have become in their own way technical and specialized, focusing on the technical skills of communication or counseling or administration. Insights for these courses are often borrowed from the related professional fields of communications or psychology or business administration, and their theological and religious aims and rationale have begun to disappear. The final consequence of the separation of theory and practice is the "detheologizing" of divinity school and seminary education.

166

It is scarcely surprising, then, that seminary and divinity school students complain that practical courses lack intellectual rigor and that scholarly courses seem irrelevant to their vocational and professional goals. The classical model for American theological education creates an enormous gap between the academic and practical aspects of a ministerial curriculum. Just as important, this standard model eliminates theology from the core of both practical and academic studies. Theology as a theoretical discipline appears disconnected from the skills needed to be a successful parish pastor. Theology as an inquiry emerging from faith and piety appears to lack the marks of an impartial and critical discipline.

In order to address the problem of integration within the theological disciplines, in order to begin to develop standards of excellence for theological scholarship, we need to reassess the capacity of theology to unify theory and practice, critical studies and pastoral concerns. *Theology can, and I believe must, regain its status as a significant critical inquiry within the church, within the university, and within our broader cultural and public life.* A recognition of theology as a critical inquiry emerging out of deeply held religious convictions can greatly enrich the cultural, intellectual, and spiritual life of our society. A restoration of theology to a central point in divinity school and seminary curricula can help us to overcome the gap between the academic and ministerial, between the scholarly and pastoral, that so bedevils American theological education. And finally, the reestablishment of theology at the center of our common intellectual and spiritual task might allow us to perceive the future directions of theological scholarship.

We can begin addressing these issues by articulating a broader and more inclusive understanding of theology. We need to recover a sense of theology as a generic term, describing not simply one discipline among others but the common task in which we are all engaged, whether in biblical studies, constructive theology, historical studies, or comparative religion. Theology rightly conceived is a *communal, formative, critical,* and *public* activity that can serve both as the integrative factor in seminary teaching, and as a key link to the rest of the university and the wider society. That is a rather sweeping claim, so I will highlight each of the elements within this definition.

Theology is a communal activity. Theology has traditionally been understood as an activity of religious communities, as faith seeking understanding. Yet the notion of community that has undergirded that view of theology has been narrowly and exclusively defined. Among modern theologians, the community of faith has been essentially defined as the community of elite, male, Anglo-European clerics. The effects of this narrow definition of community have been manifold. Women and people of color have been effectively eliminated from participating in the conversation that serves to define the nature and goals of the community. Theological discourse has become the language of elites, having little relevance either for the congregations of practicing religious people or for the broader secularized society. The marginalization of theology within our culture has been aided and abetted by this narrow definition of the community of faith.

During the last two decades, various liberation movements have demanded greater inclusiveness within religious communities. These movements have met partial success, and religious communities and their governing hierarchies have certainly become far more diverse. Nonetheless, traditional patterns of domination and subjugation continue to reign within religious and educational institutions; therefore, the situation of traditionally disadvantaged groups remains precarious. That is why the kind of community that exists at theological institutions is so important.

We are embarked on a bold experiment, dedicated to the belief that institutions that seek to represent the cultural and religious pluralism of our world can still function as intellectual and spiritual communities. Our traditions of open and unbiased inquiry have been extended to include voices not previously heard in the academic and theological conversation. We strive to be communities in which the conversation is rigorous yet open, critical yet candid. We cannot claim to be ideal communities of discourse, free from systematically distorted speech. But we can claim that we are seeking to construct an environment in which serious and thoughtful arguments, coming from diverse speakers and traditions, are given equal footing in our theological discussions.

One important contribution of this diverse and occasionally cacophonous environment is that we are guarded against succumbing to a false ideal of community. Too often we think of community as a notion limited to those groups of people who share a common history and a set of well-defined beliefs and aims. Although communities must have some aims that they hold in common, their diversity and disagreements are signs that they are living and vibrant. True communities are, in Alasdair MacIntyre's useful phrase, "historically extended, socially embodied argument(s),[1] arguments precisely about those aims and goods the community should seek. Theological thinking within such a community is inescapably temporal. Theology is a thoroughly historical discipline that does its work in the midst of communities and their traditions. Such a theology acknowledges the diversity of faith's expressions and the pluralistic environment within which faith must operate. It sees temporality as a crucial dimension of faith as a living, developing social phenomenon and accepts the culturally conditioned character of all human knowledge (including the knowledge of faith) as a sign that the transcendent God has become incarnate in human history and culture. Theology, then, is the discourse by which the arguments of these diverse perspectives are voiced.

As we seek to define criteria of excellence within our diverse theological communities, we must seek to develop genuine communities of discourse in which people of differing and even conflicting points of view engage in critical conversation with one another. The greatest danger we all face is that our diversity will lead to fragmentation—to the creation of separate communities of discourse, each locked into its own subworld of reality within its own standards of judgment. Such a development would both undermine the coherence of the theological task and make serious conversation with those outside theology increasingly unlikely. Those of us with administrative responsibility must seek to create an intellectual atmosphere in which there is an open and candid exchange of ideas. Such exchange will occasionally be sharp and contentious, but it is only within that kind of honest, if somewhat painful, conversation that a consensus about our standards of excellence can emerge. Failure to develop such critical dialogue will, I fear, yield a rather bleak future for theological scholarship.

Theology is a formative activity. Theology is, quite clearly, a reflective and cognitive activity. And yet it is a peculiar form of cognitive reflection, because its goal is not simply the further expansion of knowledge. Theology seeks a quite practical goal, what I would call the formation of religious identity.

It is a commonplace to observe that human identity is formed within the matrix of roles and structures that constitute a society. Our *identities* are formed precisely as we *identify* with the various social forms that bestow meaning on a society and its participants. Religious communities have traditionally played an important role in the process of identity formation, a role sufficiently central to socialization in Western cultures that Kant and Schleiermacher could, as we have seen, still argue in the nineteenth century for the social necessity of religion. More recently, religious communities have exercised only marginal influence within the broader socialization process and have had a decreasing impact on the identity formation of their own members. Although there are surely multiple causes for this phenomenon, one major contributing factor has been the separation of theology from the communities and practices that form religious identity and character. It is hardly surprising that communities cut off from the critical and reflective guidance of theology have become aimless and uncertain. Nor is it surprising that theology cut off from communities of practice has become the esoteric discourse of academic elites.

Theology must once again become an activity engaged in the formation of religious identity and character. To play that role, theologians must be engaged in reflection upon religious practices. Some of those practices will be located within religious communities, whereas others may be broadly distributed within society and culture. Theologians need to attend both to the practices of congregations, for example, worship, preaching, and counseling, and to societal practices that have religious and moral dimensions, for example, political discourse, public policy decisions, behavior in the professions. By analyzing the structures and language of those practices, theologians can identify the basic convictions and value commitments operating within them and seek to subject them to analysis and criticism. In so doing, theologians can then seek to contribute to the reformation of those practices and of the human identities shaped within them. In that process, theology's most critical and analytical activity can make a direct contribution to the way human beings actually live out their lives.

Theology is a critical activity. I have already indicated that I understand theology to be a critical reflection on religious practices. If theology is to be a truly critical inquiry, then the standards according to which theologians make their critical judgments must be articulated. Given the current diversity within divinity school and seminary communities, and the broad range of practices for which our students are preparing, the task of reaching consensus about our critical standards will not be easy. But as we begin to build theological faculties for the twenty-first century, we must ask some hard questions about the future of theology. How can we continue to diversify theological education while developing rigorous standards of excellence? How can theology continue to serve the needs of the churches while it addresses broader social, cultural, and political questions? How might theology contribute to the revitalization of the churches precisely as it assumes this broader, more ambitious agenda? These and other questions about the intellectual integrity of the theological disciplines can easily be set aside as we face the more imminent challenges of recruitment, placement, and finances. But we must face these perplexing intellectual issues if we hope to secure a future for theological reflection.

Happily, we have some allies in this search for critical standards. Attention to criticism, or more technically, "critique," has always been an essential form of Marxist analysis. Neo-Marxist critical theorists have produced an impressive body of scholarship analyzing the role of critique as a form of reflection that combines theory and practice. Although much of this scholarship has been either uninterested in or downright antagonistic toward religion, I am struck by the remarkable similarities between the problems faced by Christian and Marxist scholars at the end of the twentieth century. I believe we need to engage in serious conversation with the Marxist tradition as we seek a way out of our current impasse.

Another intellectual trend that deserves attention within theology is that represented by pragmatism within American philosophy. The pragmatist tradition, more than any other school of thought within post-Enlightenment philosophy, has consciously sought to give primacy to practice in its struggle to overcome a false dichotomy between reflection and activity. It is ironic that American theologians have given so little attention to that distinctive American tradition represented by Dewey, James, Peirce, and, more recently, Richard Rorty. We have traditionally drawn our resources from the European intellectual scene or most recently from developments within the Third World. In fact, one of the most powerful resources for our task lies ready at hand in our own intellectual culture. Our failure to produce a distinctively North American theology may reside in part in our neglect of this indigenous philosophical tradition.

Finally, we need to be in conversation with developments in the field of literary criticism. Traditional theological scholarship has been text oriented, focusing on the analysis of ideas within textual traditions. Historical critical inquiry has raised sharp challenges to some of the assumptions of that scholarship with regard to the literary integrity of texts, to their historical reliability, and to the authority of textual traditions. The crisis of authority within religious communities has contributed to the confusion within theological scholarship. As we seek for new directions, we may be assisted by the important discussions occurring within literary criticism. Literary critics are acutely aware of the political dimensions of interpretation and are seeking to develop political hermeneutics appropriate to literary texts. We need to attend particularly to the debates about the "literary canon" that are raging within departments of English and comparative literature. We can both contribute to and learn from those important discussions about the structure of college and university curricula, for these debates will influence significantly the ways in which young people in America are taught to read and interpret, as well as the texts that they are encouraged to study.

Discussion of the criteria of a truly critical theology can make an important contribution to the universitywide reflection on the nature of a liberal education. As we develop our conception of theology as a critical discipline, we have an opportunity to raise new queries about the relation between the descriptive and the normative, and between the critical and moral dimensions of human understanding. In so doing, we can contribute to the ongoing discussion about the moral applications of critical thinking, but we can also pose fresh questions about the fiduciary and moral presuppositions inherent in all critical inquiry.

Theology is a public activity. Finally, we need to recapture a sense in which theology is a public activity. Throughout our history in the United States, political rhetoric has had a strong theological dimension. The presidential inaugural address is the classic genre for theo-political rhetoric. Abraham Lincoln was the master of such rhetoric and was arguably America's most significant public theologian. John F. Kennedy could also invoke theological and biblical themes in his attempt to gain public support for his policies. At the same time, analyses of Kennedy's political practice indicate that his policymaking was in no obvious way directly influenced by his religious convictions. The plight of religion in the contemporary world is that (in Peter Berger's fetching phrase) it has been reduced to public rhetoric and private virtue.

One of the most encouraging developments in the sphere of public affairs in recent years has been the American Roman Catholic bishops' pastorals on peace and economic justice. Those statements have been both praised and criticized, but they have made the important contribution of introducing overt theological discourse and analysis into the public debate. Their positions have received widespread media coverage and have elicited thoughtful responses from scholars and policymakers outside the religious community. The question remains whether their statements will have any real or lasting impact on the structure of public policy—whether they will move beyond rhetoric to influence our common public reality.

There has been a great deal of discussion in academic theology about "public theology." Most of that debate has focused on the question of whether theological arguments are available for public examination and whether theological assertions are intelligible beyond the confines of a particular religious community. Although such issues are intellectually interesting and important within a rather small circle of academic theologians, they only begin to help us address what I consider the far more important questions: Will religious convictions and theological analyses have any real impact on the way our public lives are structured? Can a truly public theology have a salutary influence on the development of public policy within a pluralistic democratic nation? The real challenge to a North American public theology is to find a way—within the social, cultural, and religious pluralism of American politics—to influence the development of public policy without seeking to construct a new Christendom or lapsing into a benign moral relativism.

I have begun my deanship at Harvard at one of the most challenging but exciting times in the history of theological education. I believe that the key to the revitalization of theological scholarship lies in the revitalization of the theological dimension of our various disciplines. If we can make some progress toward developing a more inclusive and more critical conception of theology, then we might discover that theological scholarship has a future that is of interest to those in the church, the academy, and the wider society. And then we might find ourselves engaged in a critical conversation that may have enormous significance not only for the future of scholarship but for our common human future as well.

NOTE

1. Alasdair MacIntyre, *After Virtue* (Notre Dame: University of Notre Dame Press, 1981), 207.

Index